263-27

13'

"Ireta Wilson"
"Pee Wee"

Hilda Mason
O. N. U.

SHAKESPEARE'S

JULIUS CAESAR.

WITH

INTRODUCTION, AND NOTES EXPLANATORY AND CRITICAL.

FOR USE IN SCHOOLS AND CLASSES.

BY THE

Rev. HENRY N. HUDSON, LL.D.

———————◆———————

GINN & COMPANY

BOSTON · NEW YORK · CHICAGO · LONDON ·

The Athenæum Press
GINN & COMPANY · PRO-
PRIETORS · BOSTON · U.S.A.

Mildred Kannenberg

INTRODUCTION.

———•———

History of the Play.

JULIUS CÆSAR was first printed in the folio of 1623. None of the plays in that inestimable volume have reached us with the text in a sounder and clearer state; there being few passages that give an editor any trouble, none that are very troublesome.

The Rev. Mr. Fleay, in his *Shakespeare Manual*, 1876, argues somewhat strenuously to the point that "this play, as we have it, is an abridgment of Shakespeare's play, made by Ben Jonson." In support of his theory he alleges, and truly, that Jonson did in fact exercise his hand more or less in altering and refitting other men's plays. He also points out the fact, — for such it is, — that the number of short lines or broken verses in *Julius Cæsar* is uncommonly large. And he cites several words and phrases, such as "quality and kind," "bear me hard," "chew upon this," &c., which do not occur elsewhere in Shakespeare; while the same words and phrases, or something very like them, are met with in Jonson's plays. Still more to the purpose, he adduces a passage in Act iii., scene 1, which is evidently referred to in Jonson's *Discoveries*, 1637, and which, in all probability, — as I think, — has been altered, perhaps by Jonson's hand, from what Shakespeare wrote. As the question is discussed at some length in the Critical Notes, it need not be prose-cuted further here.

Such are the main particulars urged by Mr. Fleay. His argument shows a good deal of learned diligence ; still it does not, to my mind, carry any great force, certainly is far from being conclusive, and, as the Clarendon Editor observes, is "not such as the readers of Shakespeare have a right to de-mand." Nevertheless, as, on comparing the quarto and folio copies, we find that the folio has several other plays more or less abridged, some to the extent of whole scenes ; so I think it nowise improbable that, after Shakespeare's retirement from the stage, perhaps after his death, *Julius Cæsar* may have been subjected to the same process, and for the same purpose, namely, to shorten the time of representation. If this was done, it is altogether credible that Jonson may have been the man who did it : but I fail to catch any taste of Jonson's style or any smack of his idiom in the play as it stands. So that, while conceding that he may have struck out more or less of Shakespeare's matter, still I am by no means prepared to admit that he put in any thing of his own ; though, possibly enough, in a few places, as in that already specified, he may have slightly altered Shakespeare's language.

There were several other plays on the subject of Julius Cæsar, written some before, some after, the composition of Shakespeare's play ; but, as no connection has been traced between any of these and Shakespeare's, it seems hardly worth the while to make any further notice of them.

Date of the Writing.

The time when *Julius Cæsar* was composed has been variously argued, some placing it in the middle period of the Poet's labours, others among the latest; and, as no clear contemporary notice or allusion had been produced, the question could not be positively determined. It is indeed well known that the original *Hamlet* must have been written as early as 1602; and in iii. 2, of that play Polonius says, " I did enact Julius Cæsar : I was killed in the Capitol ; Brutus killed me." As the play now in hand lays the scene of the stabbing in the Capitol, it is not improbable, to say the least, that the Poet had his own *Julius Cæsar* in mind when he wrote the passage in *Hamlet*. And that such was the case is made further credible by the fact, that Polonius speaks of himself as having enacted the part when he " play'd once in the University," and that in the title-page of the first edition of *Hamlet* we have the words, " As it hath been divers times acted by his Highness' Servants in the city of London ; as also in the two Universities of Cambridge and Oxford." Still the point cannot be affirmed with certainty ; for there were several earlier plays on the subject, and especially a Latin play on Cæsar's Death, which was performed at Oxford in 1582.

Mr. Collier argued that Shakespeare's play must have been on the stage before 1603, his reason being as follows. Drayton's *Mortimeriados* appeared in 1596. The poem was afterwards recast by the author, and published again in 1603 as *The Barons' Wars*. The recast has the following lines, which were not in the original form of the poem : —

> Such one he was, of him we boldly say,
> In whose rich soul all sovereign powers did suit;
> In whom in peace *the elements all lay*
> *So mix'd*, as none could sovereignty impute :
> That 't seem'd when Heaven his model first began,
> In him it show'd *perfection in a man.*

Here we have a striking resemblance to what Antony says of
Brutus in the play : —

> His life was gentle; and *the elements*
> *So mix'd in him*, that Nature might stand up
> And say to all the world, *This was a man.*

Mr. Collier's theory is, that Drayton, before recasting his
poem, had either seen the play in manuscript or heard it at
the theatre, and so caught and copied the language of
Shakespeare.

I confess there does not seem to me any great strength in
this argument; for the idea and even the language of the
resembling lines was so much a commonplace in the Poet's
time, that no one could claim any special right of authorship
in it. Nevertheless it is now pretty certain that the play
was written as early as 1601, Mr. Halliwell having lately produced the following from Weever's *Mirror of Martyrs*, which
was printed that year : —

> The many-headed multitude were drawn
> By Brutus' speech, that Cæsar was ambitious;
> When eloquent Mark Antony had shown
> His virtues, who but Brutus then was vicious?

As there is nothing in the history that could have suggested
this, we can only ascribe it to some acquaintance with the
play : so that the passage may be justly regarded as decisive
of the question.

The style alone of the drama led me to rest in about the
same conclusion long ago. And I the rather make something of this matter, because it involves a good exercise of
mind in discriminating the Poet's different styles; which is
a very nice art indeed, and therefore apt to render the per-
ceptions delicate and acute. It has been said that a true

taste for Shakespeare is like the creation of a special sense ; and this saying is nowhere better approved than in reference to his subtile variations of language and style. For he began with what may be described as a preponderance of the poetic element over the dramatic. As we trace his course onward, we may, I think, discover a gradual rising of the latter element into greater strength and prominence, until at last it had the former in complete subjection. Now, where positive external evidence is wanting, it is mainly from the relative strength of these elements that I argue the probable date of the writing. And it seems to me that in *Julius Cæsar* the diction is more gliding and continuous, and the imagery more round and amplified, than in the dramas known to have been of the Poet's latest period.

But these distinctive notes are of a nature to be more easily felt than described ; and to make them felt examples will best serve. Take, then, a sentence from the soliloquy of Brutus just after he has pledged himself to the conspiracy : —

> 'Tis a common proof,
> That lowliness is young ambition's ladder,
> Whereto the climber-upward turns his face ;
> But, when he once attains the upmost round,
> He then unto the ladder turns his back,
> Looks in the clouds, scorning the base degrees
> By which he did ascend.

Here we have a full, rounded period in which all the elements seem to have been adjusted, and the whole expression set in order, before any part of it was written down. The beginning foresees the end, the end remembers the beginning, and the thought and image are evolved together in an even continuous flow. The thing is indeed perfect in its way, still it is not in Shakespeare's latest and highest style. Now compare with this a passage from *The Winter's Tale :* —

> When you speak, sweet,
> I'd have you do it ever: when you sing,
> I'd have you buy and sell so; so give alms;
> Pray so; and for the ordering your affairs,
> To sing them too: when you do dance, I wish you
> A wave o' the sea, that you might ever do
> Nothing but that; move still, still so, and own
> No other function.

Here the workmanship seems to make and shape itself as it goes along, thought kindling thought, and image prompting image, and each part neither concerning itself with what has gone before, nor what is coming after. The very sweetness has a certain piercing quality, and we taste it from clause to clause, almost from word to word, as so many keen darts of poetic rapture shot forth in rapid succession. Yet the passage, notwithstanding its swift changes of imagery and motion, is perfect in unity and continuity.

Such is, I believe, a fair illustration of what has long been familiar to me as the supreme excellence of Shakespeare's ripest, strongest, and most idiomatic style. *Antony and Cleopatra* is pre-eminently rich in this quality ; but there is enough of it in *The Tempest, The Winter's Tale, Coriolanus,* and *Cymbeline,* to identify them as belonging to the same stage and period of authorship. But I can find hardly so much as an earnest of it in *Julius Cæsar ;* and nothing short of very strong positive evidence would induce me to class this drama with those, as regards the time of writing.

Historical Sources.

The historic materials of this play were drawn from *The Life of Julius Cæsar, The Life of Marcus Brutus,* and *The*

Life of Marcus Antonius, as set forth in Sir Thomas North's translation of Plutarch. This work, aptly described by Warton as "Shakespeare's storehouse of learned history," was first printed in 1579, and reprinted in 1595, 1603, and 1612, not to mention several later editions. The translation was avowedly made, not directly from the Greek, but from the French version of Jaques Amyot, Bishop of Auxerre. The book is among our richest and freshest literary monuments of that age; and, apart from the use made of it by Shakespeare, is in itself an invaluable repertory of honest, manly, idiomatic Elizabethan English. A selection, embracing such portions of the work as specially illustrate Shakespeare's plays, has lately been published, with learned and appropriate editorial furnishings, by the Rev. Walter W. Skeat, M.A. This has been of great service to me in preparing the present edition.

No abstract, nor any extracts, of the Plutarchian matter need be furnished here, as nearly all the passages drawn upon for the play are given in the foot-notes. Suffice it to say, that in most of the leading incidents the charming old Greek is minutely followed; though in divers cases those incidents are worked out with surpassing fertility of invention and art. But, besides this, in many places the Plutarchian form and order of thought, and also the very words of North's racy and delectable old English, are retained, with such an embalming for immortality as Shakespeare alone could give. — It may be well to add, that on the 13th of February, B.C. 44, the feast of Lupercalia was held, when the crown was offered to Cæsar by Antony. On the 15th of March following, Cæsar was slain. In November, B.C. 43, the Triumvirs, Octavius, Antony, and Lepidus, met on a small island near Bononia, and there made up their bloody proscription.

The overthrow of Brutus and Cassius near Philippi took place in the Fall of the next year. So that the events of the drama cover a period of something over two years and a half.

The Play rightly Named.

It has been justly observed that Shakespeare shows much judgment in the naming of his plays. From this observation, however, several critics, as Gildon and Schlegel, have excepted the play in hand, pronouncing the title a misnomer, on the ground that Brutus, and not Cæsar, is the hero of it. It is indeed true that Brutus is the hero ; nevertheless, I must insist upon it that the play is rightly named, inasmuch as Cæsar is not only the subject but also the governing power of it throughout. He is the centre and spring-head of the entire action, giving law and shape to every thing that is said and done. This is manifestly true in what occurs before his death ; and it is true in a still deeper sense afterwards, since his genius then becomes the Nemesis or retributive Providence, presiding over the whole course of the drama.

The Cæsar of Shakespeare.

The characterization of this drama in some of the parts is, I confess, not a little perplexing to me. I do not feel quite sure as to the temper of mind in which the Poet conceived some of the persons, or why he should have given them the aspect they wear in the play. For instance, Cæsar is far from being himself in these scenes ; hardly one of the speeches put into his mouth can be regarded as historically characteristic ; taken all together, they are little short of a downright caricature. As here represented, he is indeed little better than a grand, strutting piece of puff-paste ; and when he speaks, it is very much in the style of a glorious vapourer and braggart, full of lofty airs and mock-thunder; than which nothing could be further from the truth of the man, whose character, even in his faults, was as compact and solid as adamant, and at the same time as limber and ductile as the finest gold. Certain critics have seized and worked upon this, as proving that Shakespeare must have been very green in classical study, or else very careless in the use of his authorities. To my thinking it proves neither the one nor the other.

It is true, Cæsar's ambition was indeed gigantic, but none too much so, I suspect, for the mind it dwelt in; for his character in all its features was gigantic. And no man ever framed his ambition more in sympathy with the great forces of Nature, or built it upon a deeper foundation of political wisdom and insight. Now this "last infirmity of noble minds" is the only part of him that the play really sets before us; and even this we do not see as it was, because it is here severed from the constitutional peerage of his gifts and virtues; all those transcendant qualities which placed him at the summit of Roman intellect and manhood being either withheld from the scene, or thrown so far into the background, that the proper effect of them is mainly lost.

Yet we have ample proof that Shakespeare understood Cæsar thoroughly; and that he regarded him as "the noblest man that ever livèd in the tide of times." For example, in *Hamlet*, he makes Horatio, who is one of his calmest and most right-thinking characters, speak of him as "the mightiest Julius." In *Antony and Cleopatra*, again, the heroine is made to describe him as "broad-fronted Cæsar." And in *King Richard the Third*, the young Prince utters these lines: —

That Julius Cæsar was a famous man:
With what his valour did enrich his wit,
His wit set down to make his valour live:
Death makes no conquest of this conqueror.

In fact, we need not go beyond Shakespeare to gather that
Julius Cæsar's was the deepest, the most versatile, and most
multitudinous head that ever figured in the political affairs of
mankind.

Indeed, it is clear from this play itself that the Poet's course
did not proceed at all from ignorance or misconception of
the man. For it is remarkable that, though Cæsar delivers
himself so out of character, yet others, both foes and friends,
deliver him much nearer the truth ; so that, while we see
almost nothing of him directly, we nevertheless get, upon
the whole, a pretty just reflection of him. Especially, in the
marvellous speeches of Antony and in the later events of the
drama, both his inward greatness and his right of mastership
over the Roman world are fully vindicated. For, in the play
as in the history, Cæsar's blood just hastens and cements
the empire which the conspirators thought to prevent. They
soon find that in the popular sympathies, and even in their
own dumb remorses, he has "left behind powers that will
work for him." He proves indeed far mightier in death
than in life ; as if his spirit were become at once the guardian angel of his cause and an avenging angel to his foes.

And so it was in fact. For nothing did so much to set
the people in love with royalty, both name and thing, as the
reflection that their beloved Cæsar, the greatest of their
national heroes, the crown and consummation of Roman
genius and character, had been murdered for aspiring to it.
Thus their hereditary aversion to kingship was all subdued
by the remembrance of how and why their Cæsar fell ; and

they who, before, would have plucked out his heart rather than he should wear a crown, would now have plucked out their own, to set a crown upon his head. Such is the natural result, when the intensities of admiration and compassion meet together in the human breast.

From all which it may well be thought that Cæsar was too great for the hero of a drama, since his greatness, if brought forward in full measure, would leave no room for any thing else, at least would preclude any proper dramatic balance and equipoise. It was only as a sort of underlying potency, or a force withdrawn into the background, that his presence was compatible with that harmony and reciprocity of several characters which a well-ordered drama requires. At all events, it is pretty clear that, where he was, such figures as Brutus and Cassius could never be very considerable, save as his assassins. They would not have been heard of in after-times, if they had not " struck the foremost man of all this world " ; in other words, the great sun of Rome had to be shorn of his beams, else so ineffectual a fire as Brutus could nowise catch the eye.

Be this as it may, I have no doubt that Shakespeare knew the whole height and compass of Cæsar's vast and varied capacity. And I sometimes regret that he did not render him as he evidently saw him, inasmuch as he alone perhaps of all the men who ever wrote could have given an adequate expression of that colossal man.

I have sometimes thought that the policy of the drama may have been to represent Cæsar, not as he was indeed, but as he must have appeared to the conspirators ; to make us see him as they saw him ; in order that they too might have fair and equal judgment at our hands. For Cæsar was literally too great to be seen by them, save as children often

see bugbears by moonlight, when their inexperienced eyes
are mocked with air. And the Poet may well have judged
that the best way to set us right towards them was by identi-
fying us more or less with them in mental position, and
making us share somewhat in their delusion. For there is
scarce any thing wherein we are so apt to err as in reference
to the characters of men when time has settled and cleared
up the questions in which they lost their way : we blame
them for not having seen as we see ; while, in truth, the
things that are so bathed in light to us were full of darkness
to them ; and we should have understood them better, had
we been in the dark along with them.

Cæsar indeed was not bewildered by the political questions
of his time ; but all the rest were, and therefore he seemed
so to them ; and while their own heads were swimming they
naturally ascribed his seeming bewilderment to a dangerous
intoxication. As for his marvellous career of success, they
attributed this mainly to his good luck ; such being the common refuge of inferior minds when they would escape the
sense of their inferiority. Hence, as generally happens with
the highest order of men, his greatness had to wait the ap-
proval of later events. He indeed, far beyond any other
man of his age, " looked into the seeds of time " ; but this
was not nor could be known, till time had developed those
seeds into their fruits. Why, then, may not the Poet's idea
have been, so to order things that the full strength of the
man should not appear in the play, as it did not in fact, till
after his fall ? This view, I am apt to think, will both explain
and justify the strange disguise — a sort of falsetto greatness
— under which Cæsar exhibits himself.

Now the seeming contradiction between Cæsar as known
and Cæsar as rendered by Shakespeare is what, more than

any thing else in the drama, perplexes me. But there is, I think, a very refined, subtile, and peculiar irony pervading this, more than any other of the Poet's plays ; not intended as such, indeed, by the speakers, but a sort of historic irony, — the irony of Providence, so to speak, or, if you please, of Fate ; much the same as is implied in the proverb, "A haughty spirit goes before a fall." This irony crops out in many places. Thus we have Cæsar most blown with arrogance and godding it in the loftiest style when the daggers of the assassins are on the very point of leaping at him. So too, all along, we find Brutus most confident in those very things where he is most at fault, or acting like a man "most ignorant of what he's most assured " ; as when he says that "Antony can do no more than Cæsar's arm when Cæsar's head is off." This, to be sure, is not meant ironically by him ; but it is turned into irony by the fact that Antony soon tears the cause of the conspirators all to pieces with his tongue. But indeed this sort of honest guile runs all through the piece as a perfusive and permeating efficacy. A still better instance of it occurs just after the murder, when the chiefs of the conspiracy are exulting in the transcendant virtue and beneficence of their deed, and in its future stage celebrity ; and Cassius says, —

> So often shall the knot of us be call'd
> The men that gave their country liberty;

and again, a little later, when Brutus says of Antony, "I know that we shall have him well to friend." Not indeed that the men themselves thought any irony in those speeches : it was natural, no doubt, that they should utter such things in all seriousness ; but what they say is interpreted into irony by the subsequent events. And when such a shallow idealist as Brutus is made to overtop and outshine the great-est practical genius the world ever saw, what is it but a re-fined and subtile irony at work on a much larger scale, and diffusing itself, secretly, it may be, but not the less vitally, into the texture? It was not the frog that thought irony, when he tried to make himself as big as the ox; but there was a pretty decided spice of irony in the mind that con-ceived the fable.

It is to be noted further, that Brutus uniformly speaks of Cæsar with respect, almost indeed with admiration. It is his ambition, not his greatness, that Brutus resents; the thought that his own consequence is impaired by Cæsar's elevation having no influence with him. With Cassius, on the con-trary, impatience of his superiority is the ruling motive: he is all the while thinking of the disparagement he suffers by Cæsar's exaltation.

> This man
> Is now become a god; and Cassius is
> A wretched creature, and must bend his body,
> If Cæsar carelessly but nod on him.
>
> Why, man, he doth bestride the narrow world
> Like a Colossus; and we petty men
> Walk under his huge legs.

Thus he overflows with mocking comparisons, and finds his pastime in flouting at Cæsar as having managed, by a sham heroism, to hoodwink the world.

And yet the Poet makes Cæsar characterize himself very much as Cassius, in his splenetic temper, describes him. Cæsar gods it in his talk, as if on purpose to approve the style in which Cassius mockingly gods him. This, taken by itself, would look as if the Poet sided with Cassius; yet one can hardly help feeling that he sympathized rather in

Antony's great oration. And the sequel, as we have seen, justifies Antony's opinion of Cæsar. Thus, it seems to me, the subsequent course of things has the effect of inverting the mockery of Cassius against himself; as much as to say "You have made fine work with your ridding the world of great Cæsar: since your daggers pricked the gas out of him, you see what a grand humbug he was."

In sober truth, the final issue of the conspiracy, as represented by Shakespeare, is a pretty conclusive argument of the blunder, not to say the crime, of its authors. Cæsar, dead, tears them and their cause all to pieces. In effect, they did but stab him into a mightier life; so that Brutus might well say, as indeed he does at last, —

> O Julius Cæsar, thou art mighty yet!
> Thy spirit walks abroad, and turns our swords
> In our own proper entrails.

Am I wrong, then, in regarding the Nemesis which asserts itself so sternly in the latter part of the play, as a reflex of irony on some of the earlier scenes? I the rather take this view, inasmuch as it infers the disguise of Cæsar to be an instance of the profound guile with which Shakespeare sometimes plays upon his characters, humouring their bent, and then leaving them to the discipline of events.*

---

* Julius Cæsar is indeed protagonist of the tragedy: but it is not the Cæsar whose bodily presence is weak, whose mind is declining in strength and sure-footed energy, — the Cæsar who stands exposed to all the accidents of fortune. It is the spirit of Cæsar which is the dominant power of the tragedy: against this — the spirit of Cæsar — Brutus fought; but Brutus, who for ever errs in practical politics, succeeded only in striking down Cæsar's body: he who had been weak now rises as pure spirit, strong and terrible, and avenges himself upon the conspirators. The contrast between the weakness of Cæsar's bodily presence in the first half of the play, and the might of his spiritual presence in the latter half, is emphasized and perhaps

The Cæsar of History.

Merivale justly affirms Julius Cæsar to be "the greatest name in history." And I believe the general verdict of mankind pronounces him at once the greatest soldier and the greatest statesman of the world. In oratory, also, he is acknowledged to have stood second only to Cicero at the time; while, as an author, he ranks among the best and highest of our Latin classics. Therewithal he was a perfect gentleman; and of the world's great military conquerors he is probably the only one to whom that title can be justly applied. All the sweetness of humanity seems to have been concentrated in his native temper and disposition. Nor were his virtues less eminent than his talents and genius; while the immense power to which he attained served, apparently, but to give his virtues larger scope and render them more conspicuous: so that his rightful seat is among the loveliest, the largest-hearted, the most magnanimous of men.

Julius Cæsar loved Rome, too, at least as well as any of his haters did, and loved her a thousand times more wisely. But it was his peculiar lot, perhaps I should rather say his special mission, to contend — alone and single-handed in the fore-front, though, to be sure, with the great body of the Roman people at his back — with the proudest, the powerfullest,

---

over-emphasized by Shakespeare. It was the error of Brutus that he failed to perceive wherein lay the true Cæsarean power, and acted with short-sighted eagerness and violence. Mark Antony, over the dead body of his lord, announces what is to follow: "Over thy wounds now do I prophesy," &c. The ghost of Cæsar, which appears on the night before the battle of Philippi, serves as a kind of visible symbol of the vast posthumous power of the Dictator. Finally, the little effort of the aristocrat republicans sinks to the ground, foiled and crushed by the force which they had hoped to abolish by one violent blow. — DOWDEN.

and the wickedest oligarchy that ever afflicted the world. This senatorial faction, small in number, but terrible in malignant activity, were, and long had been, intent on prostituting all the powers of the Roman State to their own base, selfish, sinister ends : with a few individual exceptions, they seemed to cherish the illustrious traditions of their country only as a license for their atrocious cupidity and lust. They could not be made to comprehend that either the foreign nations whom they conquered or the other classes of their own nation had any rights which they were bound to respect : practically at least, as the thing stood to their mind, all other men were created but for the one sole purpose that they might fleece them, plunder them, prey upon them. And they, they it was who were slowly murdering the liberties and the Constitution of their country, by their hideous corruption, avarice, profligacy, rapacity, inhumanity. From the very outset of his public career, Cæsar deliberately set his whole mind and bent all his matchless energies to the work of rescuing so much of the liberty and Constitution of old Rome as it was yet possible to save from the stanchless greed, the remorseless tyranny, the monstrous sensuality, which were rendering the Roman name an intolerable stench in the nostrils of Heaven and Earth. Such as they were, Cæsar wrestled with them many a long year, till he finally outwrestled and overthrew them, and thereby delivered the groaning nations from their dreadful misrule. When they could no longer meet him in open fight, they found him as wise and merciful in peace as he had been heroic and irresistible in war ; so that no means were left them for putting him down but those which they used at last, — smiles concealing daggers, kisses, to make way for stabs.

In the process of his work, this mighty man approved himself to be in no sort a philosophic enthusiast or patriotic dreamer. With his clear, healthy, practical mind, which no ideal or sentimental infatuation could get hold of, he stood face to face with men and things as they were. It was not in his line therefore to bid old "Time run back and fetch the age of gold." He knew — he would not have been Julius Cæsar if he had not known — that it was both criminal and weak to suppose that the great wicked Rome of his day was to be crushed back into the smaller and better Rome of a bygone age. If he sought to imperialize the State, and himself at its head, it was because he knew that Rome, as she then was, must have a master, and that himself was the fittest man for that office. We can all now see, what he alone saw then, that the great social and political forces of the Roman world had long been moving and converging irresistibly to that end. He was not to be deluded with the hope of reversing or postponing the issue of such deep-working causes. The great danger of the time lay in struggling to keep up a republic in show, when they already had an empire in fact. And Cæsar's statesmanship was of that high and comprehensive reach which knows better than to outface political necessities with political theories. For it is an axiom in government, no less than in science, that Nature will not be the servant of men who are too brain-sick or too proud to perceive and respect her laws. The only mode of inducing her powers to work for us is by learning their terms and letting them have their own way. There is nothing in which this holds more true than in respect of those vast moral energies which evolve and shape the life of States and empires ; and which no conscious power of man can prevent, because their working is so deep and silent as not to be known, till the results are fully prepared. Here, indeed, man's best strength is a confession of his impotence. Great Cæsar understood this matter thoroughly in reference to the political state of his time ; and his ambition, if that be the right name for it, was but the instinct of a supreme administrative faculty for administrative modes and powers answerable to the exigency. The most sagacious and far-seeing of political reformers, he was also, his enemies themselves being judges, the most gentle and benignant of civil rulers. Great faults he had indeed, measured by our standard ; but his worst vices were, in all rational and human account, preferable to the best *public* virtues of his stabbers.

As the foregoing view of Cæsar and his assassins does not tally at all points with the one commonly held, and as it may appear to some rather paradoxical, I subjoin the judgments of two learned and judicious authors, to show that I am not altogether singular. The first is from Merivale's *History of the Romans under the Empire :* —

" While other illustrious men have been reputed great for their excellence in some one department of human genius, it was declared by the concurrent voice of antiquity, that Cæsar was excellent in all. He had genius, understanding, memory, taste, reflection, industry, and exactness. ' He was great,' repeats a modern writer, ' in every thing he undertook ; as a captain, a statesman, a lawgiver, a jurist, an orator, a poet, an historian, a grammarian, a mathematician, and an architect.' The secret of his manifold excellence was discovered by Pliny in the unparalleled energy of his intellectual powers, which he could devote without distraction to several objects at once, or rush at any moment from one occupation to another with the abruptness and rapidity of lightning. Cæsar could be writing and reading, dictating and listening, all at the same time ; he was wont to occupy four amanuenses at once; and had been known, on occasions, to employ as many as seven together. And, as if to complete the picture of the most perfect specimen of human ability, we are assured that in all the exercises of the camp his vigour and skill were not less conspicuous. He fought at the most perilous moments in the ranks of the soldiers; he could manage his charger without the use of reins; and he saved his life at Alexandria by his address in the art of swimming."

The following is from a recent history of Rome by Dr. Leonard Schmitz, of Edinburgh: "The death of Cæsar was an irreparable loss, not only to the Roman people, but to the whole civilized world; for the Republic was utterly ruined, and no earthly power could restore it. Cæsar's death involved the State in fresh struggles and civil wars for many a year, until in the end it fell again (and this was the best that, under the circumstances, could have happened to it) under the supremacy of Augustus, who had neither the talent, nor the will, nor the power, to carry out all the beneficial plans which his great-uncle had formed. It has been truly said, that the murder of Cæsar was the most senseless act the Romans ever committed. Had it been possible at all to restore the Republic, it would unavoidably have fallen into the hands of a most profligate aristocracy; who would have sought nothing but their own aggrandizement; would have demoralized the people still more; and would have established their own greatness upon the ruins of their country. It is only necessary to recollect the latter years of the Republic, the depravity and corruption of the ruling classes, the scenes of violence and bloodshed which constantly occurred in the streets of Rome, to render it evident to every one that peace and security could not be restored, except by the strong hand of a sovereign;

and the Roman world would have been fortunate indeed, if it had submitted to the mild and beneficent sway of Cæsar."

The Brutus of Shakespeare.

Coleridge has a shrewd doubt as to what sort of a character the Poet meant his Brutus to be. For, in his thinking aloud just after the breaking of the conspiracy to him, Brutus avowedly grounds his purpose, not on any thing Cæsar has done, nor on what he is, but simply on what he *may become* when crowned. He "knows no personal cause to spurn at him"; nor has he "known when his affections sway'd more than his reason": but "he would be crown'd: how that might change his nature, there's the question"; and,

> since the quarrel
> Will bear no colour for the thing he is,
> Fashion it thus, — that what he is, augmented,
> Would run to these and these extremities;
> And therefore think him as a serpent's egg,
> And kill him in the shell.

So then, Brutus heads a plot to assassinate the man who, besides being clothed with the sanctions of law as the highest representative of the State, has been his personal friend and benefactor; all this, too, not on any ground of fact, but on an assumed probability that the crown will prove a sacrament of evil, and transform him into quite another man. A strange piece of casuistry indeed! but nowise unsuited to the spirit of a man who was to commit the gravest of crimes, purely from a misplaced virtue.

And yet the character of Brutus is full of beauty and sweetness. In all the relations of life he is upright, gentle, and pure; of a sensitiveness and delicacy of principle that cannot bosom the slightest stain; his mind enriched and fortified with the best extractions of philosophy; a man adorned with all the virtues which, in public and private, at home and in the circle of friends, win respect and charm the heart.

Being such a man, of course he could only do what he did under some sort of delusion. And so indeed it is. Yet this very delusion serves, apparently, to ennoble and beautify him, as it takes him and works upon him through his virtues. At heart he is a real patriot, every inch of him. But his patriotism, besides being somewhat hidebound with patrician pride, is of the speculative kind, and dwells, where his whole character has been chiefly formed, in a world of poetical and philosophic ideals. He is an enthusiastic student of books. Plato is his favourite teacher; and he has studiously framed his life and tuned his thoughts to the grand and pure conceptions won from that all but divine source : Plato's genius walks with him in the Senate, sits with him at the fireside, goes with him to the wars, and still hovers about his tent.

His great fault, then, lies in supposing it his duty to be meddling with things that he does not understand. Conscious of high thoughts and just desires, but with no gift of practical insight, he is ill fitted to "grind among the iron facts of life." In truth, he does not really see where he is ; the actual circumstances and tendencies amidst which he lives are as a book written in a language he cannot read. The characters of those who act with him are too far below the region of his principles and habitual thinkings for him to take the true cast of them. Himself incapable of such motives as govern them, he just projects and suspends his ideals in them, and then misreckons upon them as realizing the men of his own brain. So, also, he clings to the idea of the great and free republic of his fathers, the old Rome that has ever stood to his feelings touched with the consecrations of time, and glorified with the high virtues that have grown up under her cherishing. But, in the long reign of tearing faction and civil butchery, that which he worships has been substantially changed, the reality lost. Cæsar, already clothed with the title and the power of Imperator for life, would change the form so as to agree with the substance, the name so as to fit the thing. But Brutus is so filled with the idea of that which has thus passed away never to return, that he thinks to save or recover the whole by preventing such formal and nominal change.

And so his whole course is that of one acting on his own ideas, not on the facts that are before and around him. Indeed he does not *see* them ; he merely dreams his own meaning into them. He is swift to do that by which he thinks his country *ought to be benefited*. As the killing of Cæsar stands in his purpose, he and his associates are to be "sacrificers, not butchers." But, in order to any such effect as he hopes for, his countrymen generally must regard the act in the same light as he intends it. That they will do this, is the very thing which he has *in fact* no reason to conclude ; notwithstanding, because it is so *in his idea*, therefore he trusts that the conspirators will "be called purgers, not murderers." Meanwhile the plain truth is, that, if his countrymen had been capable of regarding the deed as a sacrifice, they would not have made nor permitted any occasion for it. It is certain that unless so construed the act must prove fruitful of evil : all Rome is full of things proving that it cannot be so construed ; but this is what Brutus has no eye to see.

So too, in his oration "to show the *reason* of our Cæsar's death," he speaks, in calm and dispassionate manner, just

those things which he thinks ought to set the people right,
and himself right in their eyes; forgetting all the while that
the deed cannot fail to make the people mad, and that popular madness is not a thing to be reasoned with. And for
the same cause he insists on sparing Antony, and on permit-
ting him to speak in Cæsar's funeral. To do otherwise
would be unjust, and so would overthrow the whole nature
of the enterprise as it lives in his mind. And, because in
his idea it ought so to be, he trusts that Antony will make
Cæsar's death the occasion of strengthening those who killed
him; not perceiving the strong likelihood, which soon passes
into a fact, that in cutting off Cæsar they have taken away
the only check on Antony's ambition. He ought to have
foreseen that Antony, instead of being drawn to their side,
would rather make love to Cæsar's place at their expense.

Thus the course of Brutus serves no end but to set on foot
another civil war, which naturally hastens and assures the
very thing he sought to prevent. He confides in the good-
ness of his cause, not considering that the better the cause,
the worse its chance with bad men. He thinks it safe to
trust others, because he knows they can safely trust him;
the singleness of his own eye causing him to believe that
others will see as he sees, the purity of his own heart, that
others will feel as he feels.

Here then we have a strong instance of a very good man
doing a very bad thing; and, withal, of a wise man acting
most unwisely, because his wisdom knew not its place; a
right noble, just, heroic spirit bearing directly athwart the
virtues he worships. On the whole, it is not wonderful that
Brutus should have exclaimed, as he is said to have done,
that he had worshipped Virtue, and found her at last but a
shade. So worshipped, she may well prove a shade indeed!

Admiration of the man's character, reprobation of his pro-
ceedings, — which of these is the stronger with us? And
there is, I think, much the same irony in the representation
of Brutus as in that of Cæsar; only the order of it is here
reversed. As if one should say, "O yes, yes! in the practical affairs of mankind your charming wisdom of the closet
will doubtless put to shame the workings of mere practical
insight and sagacity."

Shakespeare's exactness in the minutest details of character is well shown in the speech already referred to; which
is the utterance of a man philosophizing most unphilosophi-
cally; as if the Academy should betake itself to the stump,
and this too without any sense of the incongruity. Plutarch has a short passage which served as a hint, not indeed
for the matter, but for the style of that speech. "They do
note," says he, "that in some of his epistles he counterfeited
that brief compendious manner of the Lacedæmonians. As,
when the war was begun, he wrote to the Pergamenians in this
sort: 'I understand you have given Dolabella money: if
you have done it willingly, you confess you have offended
me; if against your wills, show it by giving me willingly.'
This was Brutus's manner of letters, which were honoured for
their briefness." The speech in question is far enough indeed from being a model of style either for oratory or any
thing else; but it is finely characteristic; while its studied
primness and epigrammatic finish contrast most unfavourably
with the frank-hearted yet artful eloquence of Antony.

And what a rare significance attaches to the brief scene of
Brutus and his drowsy boy Lucius in camp a little before the
catastrophe! There, in the deep of the night, long after all
the rest have lost themselves in sleep, and when the anxie-
ties of the issue are crowding upon him, — there we have the

earnest, thoughtful Brutus hungering intensely for the repasts
of treasured thought.

> Look, Lucius, here's the book I sought for so ;
> I put it in the pocket of my gown.

What the man is, and where he ought to be, is all signified
in these two lines.   And do we not taste a dash of benignant irony in the implied repugnance between the spirit of
the man and the stuff of his present undertaking?   The idea
of a bookworm riding the whirlwind of war !   The thing is
most like Brutus ; but how out of his element, how unsphered
from his right place, it shows him !   There is a touch of
drollery in the contrast, which the richest steeping of poetry
does not disguise.   I fancy the Poet to have been in a
bland intellectual smile, as he wrote that strain of loving ear-
nestness in which the matter is delivered.   And the irony is
all the more delectable for being so remote and unpro-
nounced ; like one of those choice arrangements in the background of a painting, which, without attracting conscious notice, give a zest and relish to what stands in front.   The
scene, whether for charm of sentiment or felicity of concep-
tion, is one of the finest in Shakespeare.   Here too he had
a hint from Plutarch : " Whilst Brutus was in the war, and
his head over-busily occupied, having slumbered a little
after supper, he spent the rest of the night in dispatching
his weightiest causes ; and if he had any leisure left, he
would read some book till the third watch of the night."   I
must add a part of what Brutus says when Lucius falls asleep
in the midst of his song : —

> This is a sleepy tune. — O murderous slumber !
> Lay'st thou thy leaden mace upon my boy
> That plays thee music ? — Gentle knave, good night ;
> I will not do thee so much wrong to wake thee :

If thou dost nod, thou break'st thy instrument;
I'll take it from thee; and, good boy, good night. —
Let me see, let me see: is not the leaf turn'd down,
Where I left reading ? Here it is, I think.

It is but right to add that, in the war between Pompey and Cæsar, Brutus, after much vacillation, sided with the former ; and, when Pompey's cause was wrecked at Pharsalia, he was one of the first to throw himself on Cæsar's clemency ; who thereupon took him to his bosom ; thus behaving with that mixture of far-sightedness and kind-heartedness which is rightly called magnanimity ; and as thinking it nobler to charm the hostility out of his enemies than to make them feel his power. These facts, to be sure, are not brought forward in the play, but the sense of them is ; and this too in a way that tells powerfully against the course of Brutus.

Such, to my apprehension, is the Brutus of Shakespeare. But the Brutus of history was neither so immaculate in purpose nor so amiable in temper as the Poet's delineation may lead us to suppose. Merivale, who is among the calmest, fairest, and solidest of English historians, has the following in reference to him : —

" He was the son of a father of the same name, who had been a prominent supporter of the Marian party, and finally lost his life by rashly joining in the enterprise of Lepidus. His mother Servilia was half-sister to Marcus Cato, and appears to have been a woman of strong character and more than usual attainments. He was born only fifteen years later than Cæsar himself. But Cæsar's intimacy with Servilia was, it may be presumed, a principal cause of the marked favour with which he distinguished her offspring.

" The elder Brutus being cut off prematurely, when his son

was only eight years of age, the care of his education passed into the hands of his uncle Cato ; and the youth became early initiated in the maxims of the Stoic philosophy, and learned to regard his preceptor, whose daughter Portia he married, as the purest model of practical and abstract virtue. But, together with many honourable and noble sentiments, he imbibed also from him that morose strictness in the exaction as well as the discharge of legal obligations which, while it is often mistaken for a guaranty of probity, is not incompatible with actual laxity of principle.

" Accordingly, we find that while, on the one hand, he refrained as a provincial officer from extorting by fraud or violence the objects of his cupidity, he was, on the other, not the less unscrupulous in demanding exorbitant interest for loans advanced to the natives, and enforcing payment with rigid pertinacity. His base transactions with the magistrates of Salamis, as also with Ariobarzanes, King of Cappadocia, are detailed in Cicero's correspondence with Atticus. It was some years after his residence in Cyprus that he commissioned a person named Scaptius to collect his debts with their accumulated interest. He allowed his agent to urge the most questionable interpretations of the law, and to enforce a rate of interest beyond what Cicero considered either legal or equitable. Scaptius, in his zeal for his employer, obtained the services of a troop of horse, with which he shut up the Salaminian Senators in their house of assembly till five of them died of starvation, being really unable to procure the sum required. The bitter reflections which Cicero makes upon the conduct of Brutus mark the strong contrast between the tried and practical friend of virtue and the pedantic aspirant to philosophic renown."

Brutus and Cassius.

The characters of Brutus and Cassius are very nicely dis-
criminated, scarce a word falling from either but what smacks
of the man. Cassius is much the better conspirator, but
much the worse man ; and the better in that because the
worse in this. For Brutus engages in the conspiracy on
grounds of abstract and ideal justice ; while Cassius holds
it both a wrong and a blunder to go about such a thing
without making success his first care. This, accordingly, is
what he works for, being reckless of all other considerations
in his choice and use of means. Withal he is more impul-
sive and quick than Brutus, because less under the self-
discipline of moral principle. His motives, too, are of a
much more mixed and various quality, because his habits
of thinking and acting have grown by the measures of experience : he studies to understand men as they are ; Brutus,
as he thinks they ought to be. Hence, in every case where
Brutus crosses him, Brutus is wrong, and he is right, — right,
that is, if success be their aim. Cassius judges, and rightly,
I think, that the end should give law to the means ; and that
" the honourable men whose daggers have stabb'd Cæsar "
should not be hampered much with conscientious scruples.

Still Brutus overawes him by his moral energy and elevation of character, and by the open-faced rectitude and purity
of his principles. Brutus has no thoughts or aims that he is
afraid or ashamed to avow ; Cassius has many which he
would fain hide even from himself. And he catches a sort
of inspiration and is raised above himself by contact with
Brutus. And Cassius, moreover, acts very much from personal hatred of Cæsar, as remembering how, not long before,
he and Brutus had stood for the chief Prætorship of the city,

and Brutus through Cæsar's favour had got the election.
And so the Poet read in Plutarch that "Cassius, being a
choleric man, and hating Cæsar privately more than he did
the tyranny openly, incensed Brutus against him." The
effect of this is finely worked out by the Poet in the man's
affected scorn of Cæsar, and in the scoffing humour in which
he loves to speak of him. For such is the natural language
of a masked revenge.

The tone of Cassius is further indicated, and with exquisite art, in his soliloquy where, after tempering Brutus to his
purpose, and finding how his "honourable metal may be
wrought," he gently slurs him for being practicable to flatteries, and then proceeds to ruminate the scheme for working
upon his vanity, and thereby drawing him into the conspiracy ; thus spilling the significant fact, that his own honour
does not stick to practise the arts by which he thinks it is a
shame to be seduced.

It is a noteworthy point also, that Cassius is too practical
and too much of a politician to see any ghosts. Acting on
far lower principles than his leader, and such as that leader
would spurn as both wicked and base, he therefore does no
violence to his heart in screwing it to the work he takes in
hand : his heart is even more at home in the work than his
head : whereas Brutus, from the wrenching his heart has suffered, keeps reverting to the moral complexion of his first
step. The remembrance of this is a thorn in his side ; while
Cassius has no sensibilities of nature for such compunctions
to stick upon. Brutus is never thoroughly himself after the
assassination : that his heart is ill at ease, is shown in a certain dogged tenacity of honour and overstraining of rectitude,
as if he were struggling to make atonement with his conscience. The stab he gave Cæsar planted in his own up-

right and gentle nature a germ of remorse, which, gathering strength from every subsequent adversity, came to embody itself in imaginary sights and sounds; the Spirit of Justice, made an ill angel to him by his own sense of wrong, hovering in the background of his after-life, and haunting his solitary moments in the shape of Cæsar's ghost. And so it is well done, that he is made to see the "monstrous apparition" just after his heart has been pierced through with many sorrows at hearing of Portia's shocking death.

Character of Portia.

The delineation of Portia is completed in a few brief masterly strokes. Once seen, the portrait ever after lives an old and dear acquaintance of the reader's inner man. Like some women I have known, Portia has strength enough to do and suffer for others, but very little for herself. As the daughter of Cato and the wife of Brutus, she has set in her eye a pattern of how she ought to think and act, being "so father'd and husbanded"; but still her head floats merged over the ears in her heart; and it is only when affection speaks that her spirit is hushed into the listening which she would fain yield only to the speech of reason. She has a clear idea of the stoical calmness and fortitude which appears so noble and so graceful in her Brutus; it all lies faithfully reproduced in her mind; she knows well how to honour and admire it; yet she cannot work it into the texture of her character; she can talk it like a book, but she tries in vain to live it.

Plutarch gives one most touching incident respecting her which the Poet did not use, though he transfused the sense of it into his work. It occurred some time after Cæsar's death, and when the civil war was growing to a head: "Brutus, seeing the state of Rome would be utterly overthrown, went to the city of Elea standing by the sea. There Portia, being ready to depart from her husband and return to Rome, did what she could to dissemble the sorrow she felt. But a certain painting bewrayed her in the end. The device was taken out of the Greek stories, how Andromache accompanied her husband Hector when he went out of Troy to the wars, and how Hector delivered her his little son, and how her eyes were never off him. Portia, seeing this picture, and likening herself to be in the same case, fell a-weeping; and coming thither oftentimes in a day to see it, she wept still." The force of this incident is indeed all reproduced in the Portia of the play; we have its full effect in the matter about her self-inflicted wound as compared with her subsequent demeanour; still I cannot help wishing the Poet had made use of the incident itself.

Portia gives herself that gash without flinching, and bears it without a murmur, as an exercise and proof of manly fortitude; and she translates her pains into smiles, all to comfort and support her husband. So long as this purpose lends her strength, she is fully equal to her thought, because here her heart keeps touch perfectly with her head. But, this motive gone, the weakness, if it be not rather the strength, of her woman's nature rushes full upon her; her feelings rise into an uncontrollable flutter, and run out at every joint and motion of her body; and nothing can arrest the inward mutiny till affection again whispers her into composure, lest she spill something that may hurt or endanger her Brutus. O noble Portia! Well might the poet Campbell say, "For the picture of that wedded pair, at once august and tender, human nature and the dignity of conjugal faith are indebted."

Mark Antony.

A rounded analysis of Antony belongs to a later period, when his native aptitudes for vice were warmed into full development by the charms of the great Egyptian sorceress; and only a few of his points as set forth in this play call for present notice. His unreserved adulation of Cæsar, and reckless purveying to Cæsar's dangerous weakness in craving to be called a king when he already had far more than kingly power, and while the obvious part of a friend was to warn him from it and help him against it, — this is wisely retained by the Poet as one of Antony's characteristic traits. Then too we have apt indications here and there of his proneness to those vicious levities and debasing luxuries which afterwards ripened into such a gigantic profligacy. He has not yet attained to that rank and full-blown combination of cruelty, perfidy, and voluptuousness, which the world associates with his name, but he is plainly on the way to it. His profound and wily dissimulation, while knitting up the hollow truce with the assassins on the very spot where "great Cæsar fell," is managed with admirable skill; his deep spasms of grief being worked out in just the right way to quench their suspicions, and make them run into the toils, when he calls on them to render him their bloody hands. Nor have they any right to complain, for he is but paying them in their own coin; and we think none the worse of him, that he fairly outdoes them at their own practice.

But Antony's worst parts as here delivered are his exultant treachery in proposing to use his colleague Lepidus as at once the pack-horse and the scape-goat of the Triumvirate, and his remorseless savagery in arranging for the slaughter of all that was most illustrious in Rome, bartering away his own uncle, to glut his revenge with the blood of Cicero ; though even here his revenge was less hideous than the cold-blooded policy of young Octavius. Yet Antony has in the play, as he had in fact, some right-noble streaks in him ; for his character was a very mixed one ; and there was to the last a fierce war of good and evil within him. Especially he had an eye to see, a heart to feel, and a soul to honour the superb structure of manhood which Rome possessed in Julius Cæsar, who stood to him indeed as a kind of superior nature, to raise him above himself. He "fear'd Cæsar, honour'd him, and loved him" ; and this religious gravitation towards him was honourable to them both. Antony's usual style of oratory is said to have been rather of the bloated and gassy sort ; yet, with the murdered Cæsar for his theme, he was for once inspired and kindled to a rapture of the truest, noblest, most overwhelming eloquence ; his actual performance being hardly exaggerated by the oration Shakespeare puts in his mouth. Nor must I omit the grateful remembrance at last of his obligations to Brutus for having saved him from the daggers of the conspirators.

The People.

That many-headed, but withal big-souled creature, the multitude, is charmingly characterized in these scenes. It is true, they are rather easily swayed hither and thither by the contagion of sympathy and of persuasive speech; yet their feelings are in the main right, and even their judgment in the long run is better than that of the pampered Roman aristocracy, inasmuch as it proceeds more from the instincts of manhood. Shakespeare evidently loved to play with the natural, unsophisticated, though somewhat childish heart of the people ; but his playing is always genial and human-hearted, with a certain angelic humour in it that seldom fails to warm us towards the subject. On the whole, he understood the people well, and they have well repaid him in understanding him better, I suspect, than the critics have done. The cobbler's droll humour, at the opening of this play, followed as it is by a strain of the loftiest poetry, is aptly noted by Campbell as showing that the Poet, "even in dealing with classical subjects, laughed at the classic fear of putting the ludicrous and sublime into juxtaposition."

General Remarks.

As a whole, this play is several degrees inferior to *Coriolanus*. Admirable as is the characterization, regarded individually, still, in respect of dramatic composition, the play does not, to my mind, stand among the Poet's masterpieces. But it abounds in particular scenes and passages fraught with the highest virtue of his genius. Among these may be specially mentioned the second scene of the first Act, where Cassius lays the egg of the conspiracy in Brutus's mind, warmed with such a wrappage of instigation as to assure its being quickly hatched. Also, the first scene of the second Act, unfolding the birth of the conspiracy, and winding up with the interview, so charged with domestic glory, of Brutus and Portia. The oration of Antony in Cæsar's funeral is such an interfusion of art and passion as realizes the very perfection of its kind. Adapted at once to the comprehension of the lowest mind and to the delectation of the highest, and running its pathos into the very quick of them that hear it, it tells with terrible effect on the people ; and when it is done we feel that Cæsar's bleeding wounds are mightier than ever his genius and fortune were. The quarrel of Brutus and Cassius is deservedly celebrated. Dr. Johnson thought it "somewhat cold and unaffecting." Coleridge thought otherwise. "I know," says he, "no part of Shakespeare that more impresses on me the belief of his genius being superhuman than this scene." I am content to err with Coleridge here, if it be an error. But there is nothing in the play that seems to me more divinely touched than the brief scene, already noticed, of Brutus and his boy Lucius. And what a dear little fellow Lucius is ! so gentle, so dutiful, so loving, so thoughtful and careful for his master ; and yet himself no more conscious of his virtue than a flower of its fragrance. His falling asleep in the midst of his song, and his exclaiming on being aroused, "The strings, my lord, are false," are so good that I cannot speak of them.

Balances & contrasts.

Brutus vs Cassius.
Antony & Octavius.
Por.   "   Cal.
Cal & Cae   "   Por. & Bru.
The consp.   "   Trumvirs
Bru. & Lucius in orchard vs B. & L. in tent.
Soothsayer vs. Gort
Bru's speech vs Antony's
Flav: vs. Marullus

JULIUS CÆSAR.

PERSONS REPRESENTED.

JULIUS CÆSAR.
OCTAVIUS CÆSAR, }
MARCUS ANTONIUS, } Triumvirs,
M. ÆMIL. LEPIDUS, } after his Death.
CICERO, PUBLIUS, POPILIUS LENA, Senators.
MARCUS BRUTUS, }
CASSIUS, }
CASCA, }
TREBONIUS, } Conspirators
LIGARIUS, } against
DECIUS BRUTUS, } Cæsar.
METELLUS CIMBER, }
CINNA, }

FLAVIUS and MARULLUS, Tribunes.
ARTEMIDORUS, a Sophist of Cnidos.
A Soothsayer.
CINNA, a Poet. Another Poet.
LUCILIUS, TITINIUS, MESSALA, young CATO, and VOLUMNIUS, Friends to Brutus and Cassius.
VARRO, CLITUS, CLAUDIUS, STRATO, LUCIUS, DARDANIUS, Servants to Brutus.
PINDARUS, Servant to Cassius.

CALPURNIA, Wife to Cæsar.
PORTIA, Wife to Brutus.

Senators, Citizens, Guards, Attendants, &c.

SCENE, *during a great part of the Play, at Rome ; afterwards at Sardis ; and near Philippi.*

ACT I.

SCENE I. — *Rome.   A Street.*

Enter FLAVIUS, MARULLUS, *and a Throng of* Citizens.

Flav. Hence ! home, you idle creatures, get you home !
Is this a holiday ?   What ! know you not,

Being mechanical,[1] you ought not walk[2]
Upon a labouring-day without the sign
Of your profession?[3] — Speak, what trade art thou?

1 Cit. Why, sir, a carpenter.

Mar. Where is thy leather apron and thy rule?
What dost thou with thy best apparel on? —
You, sir; what trade are you?

2 Cit. Truly, sir, in respect of[4] a fine workman, I am
but, as you would say, a cobbler.

Mar. But what trade art thou? Answer me directly.[5]

2 Cit. A trade, sir, that I hope I may use with a safe
conscience; which is indeed, sir, a mender of bad soles.

Mar. What trade, thou knave? thou naughty knave, what
trade?

2 Cit. Nay, I beseech you, sir, be not out with me: yet,
if you be out, sir, I can mend you.[6]

---

[1] Shakespeare often uses adjectives with the sense of plural substantives;
as *mechanical* here for *mechanics* or *artizans.* So in *Hamlet,* i. 1: "Tell me
why this same strict and most observant watch so nightly toils the *subject* of
the land." The sense in the text is, "Know you not that, being mechanics,
you ought not," &c.

[2] "Ought not *to* walk," of course. This omission of *to* is not unfrequent.
So in *The Merchant,* i. 3: "Whose own hard dealing teaches them suspect
the thoughts of others."

[3] The Poet here transfers to Rome the English customs and usages of
his own time; representing men in the several mechanic trades as having
their guilds, with appropriate regulations and badges.

[4] Here, as often, *in respect of* is equivalent to *in comparison with.* So in
the 39th Psalm of *The Psalter:* "Thou hast made my days as it were a span
long, and mine age is even as nothing *in respect of* Thee." See, also, *Hamlet,* page 219, note 29.

[5] *Cobbler,* it seems, was used of a coarse workman, or a *botcher,* in any
mechanical trade. So that the Cobbler's answer does not give the information required. — *Directly* here has the sense of the Latin *directus; in a
straightforward manner,* or *without evasion.*

[6] Of course there is a play upon the two senses of *out* here. To be *out*

Mar. What mean'st thou by that? Mend me, thou saucy fellow!

2 Cit. Why, sir, cobble you.

Flav. Thou art a cobbler, art thou?

2 Cit. Truly, sir, all that I live by is with the awl : I meddle with no tradesman's matters, nor women's matters, but with all. I am indeed, sir, a surgeon to old shoes; when they are in great danger, I re-cover them. As proper⁷ men as ever trod upon neat's-leather⁸ have gone upon my handiwork.

Flav. But wherefore art not in thy shop to-day? Why dost thou lead these men about the streets?

2 Cit. Truly, sir, to wear out their shoes, to get myself into more work. But indeed, sir, we make holiday, to see Cæsar, and to rejoice in his triumph.

Mar. Wherefore rejoice? What conquest brings he home? What tributaries follow him to Rome,
To grace in captive bonds his chariot-wheels?
You blocks, you stones, you worse than senseless things!
O you hard hearts, you cruel men of Rome,
Knew you not Pompey? Many a time and oft
Have you climb'd up to walls and battlements,
To towers and windows, yea, to chimney-tops,
Your infants in your arms,⁹ and there have sat

with a man is to be *at odds* with him; to be *out at the toes* is to need a mending of one's shoes.

⁷ *Proper* for *handsome, goodly,* or *fine.* Commonly so in Shakespeare; at least when used of persons. And so, in Hebrews, xi. 23, it is said that the parents of Moses hid him "because they saw he was a *proper* child."

⁸ *Neat's-leather* is what we call *cowhide* or *calfskin. Neat* was applied to all cattle of the bovine genus. So in *The Winter's Tale,* i. 2: "The steer, the heifer, and the calf, are all call'd *neat.*" And the word is still so used in "*neat's-foot* oil."

⁹ "Your infants *being* in your arms." Ablative absolute.

The live-long day, with patient expectation,
To see great Pompey pass the streets of Rome :
And, when you saw his chariot but appear,
Have you not made an universal shout,
That [10] Tiber trembled underneath her [11] banks,
To hear the replication [12] of your sounds
Made in her concave shores?
And do you now put on your best attire?
And do you now cull out a holiday? [13]
And do you now strew flowers [14] in his way
That comes in triumph over Pompey's blood? [15]
Be gone !
Run to your houses, fall upon your knees,
Pray to the gods to intermit [16] the plague
That needs must light on this ingratitude. [17]

[10] *That* with the force of *so that* or *insomuch that*. Often so used by the writers of Shakespeare's time, and in all sorts of writing.

[11] In classical usage the divinities of rivers were gods, and not goddesses. Old English usage, however, varies ; Drayton making them mostly feminine ; Spenser, masculine.

[12] *Replication* for *echo* or *reverberation*. — Here, as often, the infinitive *to hear* is used gerundively, or like the Latin *gerund*, and so is equivalent to *at hearing*.

[13] "Do you cull out this time for a holiday?" is the meaning.

[14] *Flowers* is here a dissyllable. This and various similar words, as *bower*, *dower*, *hour*, and *power*, the Poet uses as one or two syllables, according as his verse requires. The same with *fire*, *hire*, *tire*, *year*, and divers others.

[15] The reference is to the great battle of Munda, in Spain, which took place in the Fall of the preceding year. Cæsar was now celebrating his fifth triumph, which was in honour of his final victory over the Pompeian faction. Cnæus and Sextus, the two sons of Pompey the Great, were leaders in that battle, and Cnæus perished.

[16] *Intermit* is here equivalent to *remit* ; that is, *avert*, or *turn back*.

[17] It is evident from the opening scene, that Shakespeare, even in dealing with classical subjects, laughed at the classic fear of putting the ludicrous

Flav. Go, go, good countrymen ; and, for this fault,
Assemble all the poor men of your sort ;
Draw them to Tiber banks, and weep your tears
Into the channel, till the lowest stream
Do kiss the most exalted shores [18] of all. — [*Exeunt* Citizens.
See, whêr their basest metal [19] be not moved !
They vanish tongue-tied in their guiltiness.
Go you down that way towards the Capitol ;
This way will I.   Disrobe the images,
If you do find them deck'd with ceremony. [20]

 Mar. May we do so ?
You know it is the feast of Lupercal. [21]

 Flav. It is no matter ; let no images
Be hung with Cæsar's trophies. [22]   I'll about,

and sublime into juxtaposition. After the low and farcical jests of the saucy cobbler, the eloquence of Marullus "springs upwards like a pyramid of fire." — CAMPBELL.

[18] The meaning is, "till your tears swell the river from the extreme low-water mark to the extreme high-water mark."

[19] *Whêr* for *whether*. Thus the Poet often contracts *whether* into one syllable. The contraction occurs repeatedly in this play. — In *basest metal* Shakespeare probably had *lead* in his thought. So that the meaning is, that even these men, though as *dull* and *heavy* as lead, have yet the sense to be tongue-tied with shame at their conduct.

[20] These images were the busts and statues of Cæsar, ceremoniously decked with scarfs and badges in honour of his triumph.

[21] This festival, held in honour of Lupercus, the Roman Pan, fell on the 13th of February, which month was so named from *Februus*, a surname of the god. Lupercus was, primarily, the god of shepherds, said to have been so called because he kept off the wolves. His wife Luperca was the deified she-wolf that suckled Romulus. The festival, in its original idea, was meant for religious expiation and purification, February being at that time the last month of the year.

[22] "Cæsar's trophies" are the scarfs and badges mentioned in note 20; as appears in the next scene, where it is said that the Tribunes "are put to silence for pulling scarfs off Cæsar's images."

And drive away the vulgar[23] from the streets :
So do you too, where you perceive them thick.
These growing feathers pluck'd from Cæsar's wing
Will make him fly an ordinary pitch ;[24]
Who else would soar above the view of men,
And keep us all in servile fearfulness.   [*Exeunt.*

SCENE II. — *The Same.   A Public Place.*

Enter, in Procession, with Music, CÆSAR ; ANTONY, *for the
    course ;* CALPURNIA, PORTIA, DECIUS, CICERO, BRUTUS,
    CASSIUS, *and* CASCA ; *a great Crowd following, among
    them a* Soothsayer.

Cæs. Calpurnia, —

Casca. Peace, ho ! Cæsar speaks.   [*Music ceases.*

Cæs. Calpurnia, —

Cal. Here, my lord.

Cæs. Stand you directly in Antonius' way,
When he doth run his course.[1] — Antonius, —

---

[23] The Poet often uses *vulgar* in its Latin sense of *common*. Here it
means the common people.

[24] *Pitch* is here a technical term in falconry, and means the highest flight
of a hawk or falcon.

[1] Marcus Antonius was at this time Consul, as Cæsar himself also was.
Each Roman *gens* had its own priesthood, and also its peculiar religious
rites.   The priests of the Julian gens (so named from Iulus the son of
Æneas) had lately been advanced to the same rank with those of the god
Lupercus ; and Antony was at this time at their head.   It was probably as
chief of the Julian Luperci that he officiated on this occasion in "the holy
course."— It may be well to add, here, that in old Roman society the *gens*
was much the same as the Scottish *clan* in modern times ; and that all the
individuals, both male and female, of a given gens inherited what is called
the gentilitial name ; as Julius and Julia, Antonius and Antonia, Calpurnius
and Calpurnia, Octavius and Octavia, Junius and Junia, Portius and Portia,
Cassius and Cassia, Tullius and Tullia, &c.

Ant. Cæsar, my lord?

Cæs. Forget not, in your speed, Antonius,
To touch Calpurnia; for our elders say,
The barren, touchèd in this holy chase,
Shake off their sterile curse.[2]

Anto.   I shall remember:
When Cæsar says *Do this*, it is perform'd.

Cæs. Set on; and leave no ceremony out.   [*Music.*

Sooth. Cæsar!

Cæs. Ha! who calls?

Casca. Bid every noise be still. — Peace yet again!
                                        [*Music ceases.*

Cæs. Who is it in the press that calls on me?
I hear a tongue, shriller than all the music,
Cry *Cæsar!* Speak; Cæsar is turn'd to hear.

Sooth. Beware the Ides of March.

Cæs.   What man is that?

Bru. A soothsayer bids you beware the Ides of March.[3]

Cæs. Set him before me; let me see his face.

---

[2] It was an old custom at these festivals for the priests, all naked except a girdle about the loins, to run through the streets of the city, waving in the hand a thong of goat's hide, and striking with it such women as offered themselves for the blow, in the belief that this would prevent or avert " the sterile curse." — Cæsar was at this time childless; his only daughter, Julia, married to Pompey the Great, having died some years before, upon the birth of her first child, who also died soon after. The Poet justly ascribes to Cæsar the natural desire of children to inherit his vast fame and honours; and this desire is aptly signified in the play, as such an ambition to be the founder of a royal or imperial line would be an additional motive for the conspiracy against him.

[3] Coleridge has a remark on this line, which, whether true to the subject or not, is very characteristic of the writer: " If my ear does not deceive me, the metre of this line was meant to express that sort of mild philosophic contempt, characterizing Brutus even in his first casual speech." The metrical analysis of the line is, an Iamb, two Anapests, and two Iambs.

Cass. Fellow, come from the throng; look upon Cæsar.

Cæs. What say'st thou to me now? speak once again.

Sooth. Beware the Ides of March.

Cæs. He is a dreamer; let us leave him. — Pass.

           [*Sennet.*[4]   *Exeunt all but* BRUTUS *and* CASSIUS.

Cass. Will you go see the order of the course?

Bru. Not I.

Cass. I pray you, do.

Bru. I am not gamesome:[5] I do lack some part
Of that quick spirit[6] that is in Antony.
Let me not hinder, Cassius, your desires;
I'll leave you.

    Cass. Brutus, I do observe you now of late:
I have not from your eyes that gentleness
And show of love as[7] I was wont to have:
You bear too stubborn and too strange a hand
Over your friend that loves you.[8]

    Bru.   Cassius,

---

[4] *Sennet* is an old musical term occurring repeatedly in Shakespeare; of uncertain origin, but denoting a peculiar succession of notes on a trumpet, used, as here, to signal the march of a procession.

[5] *Gamesome* is *fond of sport*, or *sportively inclined.* Repeatedly so.

[6] *Quick* for *lively* or *animated.* So we have it in the phrases, "*quick* recreation," and "*quick* and merry words." — *Spirit*, in Shakespeare, is often pronounced as one syllable, and sometimes spelt so, — *sprite, spright.*

[7] The demonstratives *this, that,* and *such,* and also the relatives *which, that,* and *as,* were often used indiscriminately. So a little later in this scene: "Under *these* hard conditions *as* this time is like to lay on us."

[8] This man, Caius Cassius Longinus, had married Junia, a sister of Brutus. Both had lately stood for the chief Prætorship of the city, and Brutus, through Cæsar's favour, had won it; though Cassius was at the same time elected one of the sixteen Prætors or judges of the city. This is said to have produced a coldness between Brutus and Cassius, so that they did not speak to each other, till this extraordinary flight of patriotism brought them together.

Be not deceived : if I have veil'd my look,
I turn the trouble of my countenance
Merely [9] upon myself.   Vexèd I am
Of late with passions of some difference, [10]
Conceptions only proper to myself,
Which give some soil, perhaps, to my behaviours ; [11]
But let not therefore my good friends be grieved, —
Among which number, Cassius, be you one, —
Nor construe [12] any further my neglect,
Than that poor Brutus, with himself at war,
Forgets the shows of love to other men.

   Cass. Then, Brutus, I have much mistook your passion ; [13]
By means whereof [14] this breast of mine hath buried
Thoughts of great value, worthy cogitations.
Tell me, good Brutus, can you see your face ?
   Bru. No, Cassius ; for the eye sees not itself
But by reflection from some other thing. [15]

---

   [9] *Merely*, here, is *altogether* or *entirely*.   A frequent usage.

   [10] That is, *conflicting* passions ; such as his love to Cæsar personally,
and his hatred of Cæsar's power in the State.

   [11] " Which blemish or tarnish the lustre of my *manners*."   The Poet repeatedly uses the plural, *behaviours*, for the particular acts which make up
what we call behaviour.   And so of several other words.

   [12] In Shakespeare, and, I think, in all other poetry, *construe* always has
the accent on the first syllable.   How or whence the present *vulgar* pro-
nunciation of it came into use, I cannot say.   The same, too, of *misconstrue*,
which always has the accent on *con*.

   [13] The Poet uses *mistook* and *mistaken* indiscriminately.   He also sometimes uses *passion* for any feeling, sentiment, or emotion, whether painful or
pleasant.   So he has " more merry tears the *passion* of loud laughter never
shed," and " free from gross *passion* or of mirth or anger."

   [14] *Means* was sometimes used in the sense of *cause* or *reason*.   *Whereof*
refers to the preceding clause.

   [15] By an image or " shadow " *reflected* from a mirror, or from water, or
some polished surface.

Cass. 'Tis just : [16]
And it is very much lamented, Brutus,
That you have no such mirror as will turn
Your hidden worthiness into your eye,
That you might see your shadow.   I have heard,
Where many of the best respect [17] in Rome, —
Except immortal Cæsar ! — speaking of Brutus,
And groaning underneath this age's yoke,
Have wish'd that noble Brutus had his eyes.

Bru.   Into what dangers would you lead me, Cassius,
That you would have me seek into myself
For that which is not in me?

Cass.   Therefore, good Brutus, be prepared to hear :
And, since you know you cannot see yourself
So well as by reflection, I, your glass,
Will modestly discover to yourself
That of yourself which you yet know not of.
And be not jealous on me, [18] gentle Brutus :
Were I a common laugher, or did use
To stale [19] with ordinary oaths my love
To every new protester ; [20] if you know

---

[16] *'Tis just* is the same as our phrase, " That's so," or " Exactly so."

[17] The sense probably is, " I have *been present* where many of the *highest repute*, or held in the highest consideration."   *Respect* was often used so. — In what follows, " Except immortal Cæsar ! " is very emphatic, and intensely ironical.

[18] *On* and *of* were used indifferently in such cases.   *Jealous*, also, for *doubtful* or *suspicious*.   So a little further on : " That you do love me, I am nothing *jealous.*"

[19] To *stale* a thing is to make it *common* or *cheap* by indiscriminate use. So in iv. 1, of this play : " Out of use, and *staled* by other men." — *Laugher*, if it be the right word, must mean *jester* or *buffoon*.   See Critical Notes.

[20] To *protest* occurs frequently in the sense of to *profess*, to *declare*, or to *vow*.   The passage is well explained by one in *Hamlet*, i. 3 : " Do not dull thy palm with entertainment of each new-hatch'd, unfledged comrade."

That I do fawn on men, and hug them hard,
And after scandal them ; or if you know
That I profess myself, in banqueting,
To all the rout,[21] then hold me dangerous.

[Flourish and shout.

Bru. What means this shouting?   I do fear the people
Choose Cæsar for their king.

Cass.   Ay, do you fear it?
Then must I think you would not have it so.

Bru. I would not, Cassius ; yet I love him well,
But wherefore do you hold me here so long?
What is it that you would impart to me?
If it be aught toward[22] the general good,
Set honour in one eye and death i' the other,
And I will look on death indifferently ;
For let the gods so speed[23] me as I love
The name of honour more than I fear death.

Cass. I know that virtue to be in you, Brutus,
As well as I do know your outward favour.[24]
Well, honour is the subject of my story.
I cannot tell what you and other men
Think of this life ; but, for my single self,
I had as lief[25] not be as live to be

---

[21] The order, according to the sense, is, "if you know that, in banquet-ing, I profess myself to all the rout." — To make his flattery work the bet-ter, Cassius here assures the "gentle Brutus" that he scorns to flatter, that he never speaks any thing but austere truth, and that he is extremely select in his friendships.

[22] Here, as often, *toward* is two syllables, with the accent on the last.

[23] To *speed* for to *prosper* or *bless;* a frequent usage. So in *The Merry Wives,* iii. 4: "Heaven so *speed* me in my time to come!"

[24] *Favour* for *look, aspect,* or *appearance,* was very common.

[25] *Lief* or *lieve* is an old word for *glad* or *willing, gladly* or *willingly;* the opposite of *loth* or *loath.* Its original sense was about the same as *dear.*

In awe of such a thing as I myself.)
I was born free as Cæsar; so were you:
We both have fed as well; and we can both
Endure the Winter's cold as well as he:
For once, upon a raw and gusty day,
The troubled Tiber chafing with her shores,
Cæsar said to me, *Darest thou, Cassius, now*
Leap in with me into this angry flood,
And swim to yonder point? Upon the word,
Accoutred as I was, I plungèd in,
And bade him follow: so indeed he did.
The torrent roar'd, and we did buffet it
With lusty sinews, throwing it aside
And stemming it with hearts of controversy:[26]
But, ere we could arrive the point[27] proposed,
Cæsar cried, *Help me, Cassius, or I sink!*
I, as Æneas, our great ancestor,
Did from the flames of Troy upon his shoulder
The old Anchises bear, so from the waves of Tiber
Did I the tirèd Cæsar: and this man
Is now become a god; and Cassius is
A wretched creature, and must bend his body,
If Cæsar carelessly but nod on him.
He had a fever when he was in Spain;[28]

[26] That is, with *opposing* or *contending* hearts; *heart* being put for *courage*. The Poet has many like expressions, as, "mind of love" for *loving mind*, "thieves of mercy" for *merciful thieves*, "time of scorn" for *scornful time*, &c.

[27] Shakespeare uses both *arrive* and *aspire* as transitive verbs, and in the sense of *reach* or *attain*. So in *3 Henry the Sixth*, v. 3: "Those powers that the Queen hath raised in Gallia have *arrived* our coast." Also Milton, in *Paradise Lost*, ii. 409: "Ere he *arrive* the happy isle."

[28] *Fever* appears to have been used for *sickness* in general, as well as for what we call a fever. Cæsar had three several campaigns in Spain at

And when the fit was on him I did mark
How he did shake : 'tis true, this god did shake :
His coward lips did from their colour fly ;[29]
And that same eye, whose bend[30] doth awe the world,
Did lose his[31] lustre. I did hear him groan :
Ay, and that tongue of his, that bade the Romans
Mark him, and write his speeches in their books,
Alas, it cried, *Give me some drink, Titinius,*
As a sick girl. — Ye gods, it doth amaze me,
A man of such a feeble temper[32] should

different periods of his life, and the text does not show which of these Shakespeare had in mind. The following from Plutarch would seem to infer that
Cæsar was first taken with the epilepsy during his third campaign, which
closed with the great battle of Munda, March 17, B.C. 45 ; but Plutarch elsewhere speaks of him as having had the disease at an earlier period : " Concerning the constitution of his body, he was lean, white, and soft-skinned,
and often subject to headache, and otherwhile to the falling-sickness ; the
which took him the first time, as it is reported, in Corduba, a city of Spain ;
but yet therefore yielded not to the disease of his body, to make it a cloak
to cherish him withal ; but, contrarily, took the pains of war as a medicine
to cure his sick body, fighting always with his disease, travelling continually, living soberly, and commonly lying abroad in the field."

[29] The image, very bold, somewhat forced, and not altogether happy, is
of a cowardly soldier running away from his flag.

[30] *Bend* for *look.* The verb to *bend,* when used of the eyes, often has the
sense of to *direct.* So in *1 Henry the Fourth,* ii. 3 : " Why dost thou *bend*
thine eyes upon the earth ? "

[31] *His* for *its,* and referring to *eye.* *Its* was not then an accepted word,
but was knocking for admission ; and Shakespeare has it several times. It
does not once occur in the English Bible as first printed in 1611 ; and only
twice, I think, in *Paradise Lost,* published in 1667.

[32] *Temper* for *constitution* or *temperament.* — " The lean and wrinkled
Cassius " venting his spite at Cæsar, by ridiculing his liability to sickness
and death, is charmingly characteristic. In fact, this mighty man, with all
his electric energy of mind and will, was of a rather fragile and delicate
make ; and his countenance, as we have it in authentic busts, is almost a
model of feminine beauty. Cicero, who did not love him at all, in one of his
Letters applies to him a Greek word, the same that is used for *miracle* or

So get the start of the majestic world,
And bear the palm alone.   [*Shout. Flourish.*

  Bru. Another general shout!
I do believe that these applauses are
For some new honours that are heap'd on Cæsar.

  Cass. Why, man, he doth bestride the narrow world
Like a Colossus;[33] and we petty men
Walk under his huge legs, and peep about
To find ourselves dishonourable graves.
Men at some time are masters of their fates:
The fault, dear Brutus, is not in our stars,[34]
But in ourselves, that we are underlings.
Brutus and *Cæsar:* what should be in that *Cæsar?*[35]
Why should that name be sounded more than yours?
Write them together, yours is as fair a name;
Sound them, it doth become the mouth as well;
Weigh them, it is as heavy; conjure with them,
Brutus will start a spirit as soon as *Cæsar.*[36]

wonder in the *New Testament;* the English of the passage being, "This
miracle (monster?) is a thing of terrible energy, swiftness, diligence."

[33] Observe the force of *narrow* here; as if Cæsar were grown so enor-
mously big that even the world seemed a little thing under him. Some
while before this, the Senate had erected a bronze statue of Cæsar, standing
on a globe, and inscribed to "Cæsar the Demigod"; which inscription,
however, Cæsar had erased. — The original Colossus was a bronze statue a
hundred and twenty feet high, set up astride a part of the harbour at Rhodes,
so that ships passed "under its huge legs."

[34] Referring to the old astrological notion of planetary influence on the
fortunes and characters of men. The Poet has many such allusions.

[35] Meaning, "what *is* there in that word *Cæsar?*" The Poet often uses
should be where we should use *is* or *can be.* So I have sometimes been
asked, "What *might* your name be?"

[36] The allusion is to the old custom of muttering certain names, supposed to have in them "the might of magic spells," in raising or conjuring
up spirits. — *Brutus* and *Cæsar* are here printed in Italic, to show that Cassius is referring to the magical power of the names, and not to the men.

Now, in the names of all the gods at once,
Upon what meat doth this our Cæsar feed,
That he is grown so great?   Age, thou art shamed!
Rome, thou hast lost the breed of noble bloods!
When went there by an age, since the great flood,[37]
But it was famed with more than with one man?
When could they say, till now, that talk'd of Rome,
That her wide walls encompass'd but one man?
Now is it Rome indeed, and room [38] enough,
When there is in it but one only man.
O, you and I have heard our fathers say
There was a Brutus once [39] that would have brook'd
Th' eternal Devil to keep his state [40] in Rome,
As easily as a king!

Bru. That you do love me, I am nothing jealous;
What you would work me to, I have some aim:[41]

---

[37] By this a Roman would of course mean Deucalion's flood.

[38] A play upon *Rome* and *room*, which appear to have been sounded more alike in Shakespeare's time than they are now. — In the next line, "but one only" is redundant or reduplicative, and means *but one*, or *only one*. Repeatedly so.

[39] Alluding to Lucius Junius Brutus, who bore a leading part in driving out the Tarquins, and in turning the Kingdom into a Republic. Afterwards, as Consul, he condemned his own sons to death for attempting to restore the Kingdom. The Marcus Junius Brutus of the play supposed himself to be lineally descended from him. His mother, Servilia, also derived her lineage from Servilius Ahala, who slew Spurius Mælius for aspiring to royalty. Merivale justly remarks that "the name of Brutus forced its possessor into prominence as soon as royalty began to be discussed."

[40] "Keep his state" may mean either preserve his dignity or set up his throne; *state* being repeatedly used for *throne*. — The Poet has *eternal* several times for *infernal*. Perhaps our Yankee phrases, "*tarnal* shame," "*tarnal* scamp," &c., are relics of this usage. It seems that the Puritans and Calvinists thought *infernal* too profane for godly mouths, and so transferred its sense to *eternal*.

[41] "Work me to" is *persuade* or *induce* me to. — *Aim* is *guess*. So the

How I have thought of this, and of these times,
I shall recount hereafter ; for this present,
I would not, so with love I might entreat you,
Be any further moved.   What you have said,
I will consider ; what you have to say,
I will with patience hear ; and find a time
Both meet to hear and answer such high things.
Till then, my noble friend, chew [42] upon this :
Brutus had rather be a villager
Than to repute himself [43] a son of Rome
Under these hard conditions as this time
Is like to lay upon us.

   Cass. I am glad that my weak words
Have struck but thus much show of fire [44] from Brutus.

   Bru. The games are done, and Cæsar is returning.

   Cass. As they pass by, pluck Casca by the sleeve ;
And he will, after his sour fashion, tell you
What hath proceeded [45] worthy note to-day.

Re-enter CÆSAR *and his Train.*

   Bru. I will do so. — But, look you, Cassius,
The angry spot doth glow on Cæsar's brow,
And all the rest look like a chidden train :
Calpurnia's cheek is pale ; and Cicero

verb in *Romeo and Juliet*, i. 1 : "I *aim'd* so near when I supposed you
loved." And the Poet has it so in divers other places.

   [42] To *chew* is, literally, to *ruminate ;* that is, *reflect* or *meditate.*

   [43] An irregular construction, but common in the Poet's time. So Bacon
in his essay *Of Friendship :* "A man were better relate himself to a statue
or picture than *to* suffer his thoughts to pass in smother."

   [44] Referring to the use of steel and flint in starting a fire. So, in *Troilus
and Cressida*, iii. 3, Thersites says of Ajax's wit, "It lies as coldly in him as
fire in a flint, which will not show without knocking."

   [45] That is, hath *happened* or *come to pass.* Repeatedly so.

Looks with such ferret [46] and such fiery eyes
As we have seen him in the Capitol,
Being cross'd in conference by some Senator.

  Cass. Casca will tell us what the matter is.

  Cæs. Antonius, —

  Ant. Cæsar?

  Cæs. Let me have men about me that are fat;
Sleek-headed men, and such as sleep o' nights:
Yond Cassius has a lean and hungry look;
He thinks too much: [47] such men are dangerous.

  Ant. Fear him not, Cæsar; he's not dangerous;
He is a noble Roman, and well given. [48]

  Cæs. Would he were fatter! but I fear him not:
Yet, if my name were liable to fear,
I do not know the man I should avoid
So soon as that spare Cassius.   He reads much;
He is a great observer, and he looks
Quite through the deeds of men: he loves no plays, [49]

---

[46] The ferret is a very ferocious little animal of the weasel kind, noted for its fire-red eyes. — The angry spot on Cæsar's brow, Calpurnia's pale cheek, and Cicero spouting fire from his eyes as when kindled by opposition in the Senate, make an exceedingly vivid picture.

[47] So in North's Plutarch, *Life of Julius Cæsar:* "When Cæsar's friends complained unto him of Antonius and Dolabella, that they pretended some mischief towards him, he answered them, As for those fat men, and smooth-combed heads, I never reckon of them; but these pale-visaged and carrion-lean people, I fear them most; meaning Brutus and Cassius."

[48] *Well given* is *well disposed.* So in North's Plutarch: "If there were any noble attempt done in all this conspiracy, they refer it wholly unto Brutus; and all the cruel and violent acts unto Cassius, who was Brutus's. familiar friend, but not so *well given* and conditioned as he."

[49] This is from Plutarch's *Life of Antonius:* "In his house they did nothing but feast, dance, and masque; and himself passed away the time in hearing of foolish plays, and in marrying these players, tumblers, jesters, and such sort of people."

As thou dost, Antony ; he hears no music :[50]
Seldom he smiles ; and smiles in such a sort
As if he mock'd himself, and scorn'd his spirit
That could be moved to smile at any thing.
Such men as he never be at heart's ease
Whiles they behold a greater than themselves ;
And therefore are they very dangerous.
I rather tell thee what is to be fear'd
Than what I fear, for always I am Cæsar.
Come on my right hand, for this ear is deaf,[51]
And tell me truly what thou think'st of him.

    [Exeunt CÆSAR *and his Train.*　CASCA *stays.*

　Casca. You pull'd me by the cloak : would you speak
with me ?

　Bru. Ay, Casca ; tell us what hath chanced to-day,
That Cæsar looks so sad.[52]

　Casca. Why, you were with him, were you not ?

　Bru. I should not then ask Casca what had chanced.

---

[50] The power of music is repeatedly celebrated by Shakespeare, and sometimes in strains that approximate the classical hyperboles about Orpheus,
Amphion, and Arion. His own ear, no doubt, was exquisitely sensitive to
"the touches of sweet harmony." What is here said of Cassius has an apt
commentary in *The Merchant of Venice,* v. 1 : —

> The man that hath no music in himself,
> Nor is not moved with concord of sweet sounds,
> Is fit for treasons, stratagems, and spoils ;
> The motions of his spirit are dull as night,
> And his affections dark as Erebus :
> Let no such man be trusted.

[51] This is one of the little touches of invention that so often impart a
fact-like vividness to the Poet's scenes ; like that remarked in note 46.

[52] *Sad* in its old sense of *grave* or *serious,* probably. A frequent usage.
So, in *Romeo and Juliet,* i. 1, Benvolio says, " Tell me in *sadness,* who 'tis
that you love " ; and Romeo replies, " In *sadness,* cousin, I do love a woman."

Casca. Why, there was a crown offer'd him ; and, being offer'd him, he put it by with the back of his hand, thus ; and then the people fell a-shouting.

Bru. What was the second noise for?

Casca. Why, for that too.

Cass. They shouted thrice : what was the last cry for?

Casca. Why, for that too.

Bru. Was the crown offer'd him thrice?

Casca. Ay, marry,[53] was't, and he put it by thrice, every time gentler than other ; and at every putting-by mine honest neighbours shouted.

Cass. Who offer'd him the crown?

Casca. Why, Antony.

Bru. Tell us the manner of it, gentle Casca.

Casca. I can as well be hang'd, as tell the manner of it : it was mere foolery ; I did not mark it. I saw Mark Antony offer him a crown ; — yet 'twas not a crown neither, 'twas one of these coronets ; — and, as I told you, he put it by once : but, for all that, to my thinking, he would fain [54] have had it. Then he offered it to him again ; then he put it by again : but, to my thinking, he was very loth to lay his fingers off it. And then he offered it the third time ; he put it the third time by ; and still, as he refused it, the rabblement shouted, and clapp'd their chopt hands, and threw up their sweaty night-caps, and uttered such a deal of stinking breath because Cæsar refused the crown, that it had almost choked Cæsar ; for he swooned, and fell down at it : and, for mine

[53] From an old custom of appealing to the Virgin Mary, *marry* grew into common use as an intensive; like *verily, indeed, to be sure.* So the Latin often has *heracle* and *edepol ;* the latter from swearing by Castor and Pollux.

[54] *Fain* is *glad* or *gladly ;* much used in the Poet's time. So in St. Luke, xv. 16: "He would *fain* have filled his belly with the husks," &c.

own part, I durst not laugh, for fear of opening my lips and receiving the bad air.[55]

Cass. But, soft![56] I pray you. What, did Cæsar swoon?

Casca. He fell down in the market-place, and foam'd at mouth, and was speechless.

Bru. 'Tis very like : he hath the falling-sickness.

Cass. No, Cæsar hath it not ; but you, and I,
And honest Casca, we have the falling-sickness.[57]

Casca. I know not what you mean by that ; but I am sure Cæsar fell down. If the tag-rag people did not clap him and hiss him, according as he pleased and displeased them, as they use to do the players in the theatre, I am no true man.[58]

---

[55] Cæsar sat to behold that sport upon the pulpit for orations, in a chain of gold, apparelled in triumphant manner. Antonius, who was Consul at that time, was one of them that ran this holy course. So when he came into the market-place the people made a lane for him to run at liberty, and he came to Cæsar, and presented him a diadem wreathed about with laurel. Whereupon there rose a certain cry of rejoicing, not very great, done only by a few appointed for the purpose. But when Cæsar refused the diadem, then all the people together made an outcry of joy. Then Antonius offering it him again, there was a second shout of joy, but yet of a few. But when Cæsar refused it again the second time, then all the whole people shouted. Cæsar having made this proof, found that the people did not like of it, and thereupon rose out of his chair, and commanded the crown to be carried unto Jupiter in the Capitol. — PLUTARCH.

[56] *Soft!* was much used as an exclamation for arresting or retarding the speed of a person or thing ; meaning about the same as *hold! stay!* or *not too fast!* So in *Othello,* v. 2 : " *Soft* you ! a word or two before you go."

[57] Meaning the disease of " standing prostrate " before Cæsar. *Falling-sickness* or *falling-evil* was the English name for epilepsy. Cæsar was subject to it, especially in his later years, as Napoleon also is said to have been. See page 50, note 28.

[58] " *True* man " is *honest* man. Often used in that sense, but especially as opposed to *thief.* So in *Cymbeline,* ii. 3 : " 'Tis gold which makes the true man kill'd, and saves the thief ; nay, sometimes hangs both thief and true man." Also in *Venus and Adonis :* " Rich preys make true men thieves."

Bru. What said he when he came unto himself?

Casca. Marry, before he fell down, when he perceived the common herd was glad he refused the crown, he pluck'd me ope his doublet,[59] and offer'd them his throat to cut : an I had been a man of any occupation,[60] if I would not have taken him at a word, I would I might go to Hell among the rogues : — and so he fell. When he came to himself again he said, if he had done or said any thing amiss, he desired their Worships to think it was his infirmity.[61] Three or four wenches, where I stood, cried, *Alas, good soul!* and forgave him with all their hearts. But there's no heed to be taken of them : if Cæsar had stabb'd their mothers, they would have done no less.

Bru. And, after that, he came thus sad away?

Casca. Ay.

Cass. Did Cicero say any thing?

Casca. Ay, he spoke Greek.

Cass. To what effect?

Casca. Nay, an I tell you that, I'll ne'er look you i' the face again : but those that understood him smiled at one

[59] *Doublet* was the common English name of a man's upper outward garment. — In this clause, *me* is simply redundant; as in Falstaff's speech in praise of sack : " It ascends *me* into the brain ; dries *me* there all the foolish and dull and crudy vapours which environ it."

[60] " A man of occupation " probably means not only a mechanic or user of cutting-tools, but also a man of business and of action, as distinguished from a gentleman of leisure, or an idler. — *An*, in this clause, is an old equivalent for *if.* Often used thus by the Poet. See *Hamlet*, page 89, note 34.

[61] Thereupon Cæsar rising departed home to his house ; and, tearing open his doublet-collar, making his neck bare, he cried out aloud to his friends, that his throat was ready to offer to any man that would come and cut it. Notwithstanding it is reported that, afterwards, to excuse his folly, he imputed it to his disease, saying that their wits are not perfect which have this disease of the falling-evil. — PLUTARCH.

another, and shook their heads ;[62] but, for mine own part, it
was Greek to me.[63]   I could tell you more news too : Marullus and Flavius, for pulling scarfs off Cæsar's images, are put
to silence.[64]   Fare you well.   There was more foolery yet,
if I could remember it.

Cass. Will you sup with me to-night, Casca?

Casca. No, I am promised forth.[65]

Cass. Will you dine with me to-morrow?

Casca. Ay, if I be alive, and your mind hold, and your
dinner worth the eating.

Cass. Good ; I will expect you.

Casca. Do so : farewell both.   [*Exit* CASCA.

Bru. What a blunt[66] fellow is this grown to be !
He was quick mettle when he went to school.

Cass. So is he now in execution
Of any bold or noble enterprise,

---

[62] A charming invention. Cicero had a long, sharp, agile tongue, and
was mighty fond of using it ; and nothing was more natural, supposing him
to have been present, than that he should snap off some keen sententious
sayings ; prudently veiling them however in a foreign language from all but
those who might safely understand them.

[63] The phrase " it is Greek to me " is still in common use for any thing
that is not understood.

[64] There were set up images of Cæsar in the city, with diadems upon
their heads like kings.   Those the two tribunes, Flavius and Marullus, went
and pulled down, and furthermore, meeting with them that first saluted
Cæsar as king, they committed them to prison.   The people followed them
rejoicing at it, and called them Brutuses, because of Brutus who had in old
times driven the kings out of Rome.   Cæsar was so offended withal, that he
deprived Marullus and Flavius of their tribuneships.— PLUTARCH.

[65] Shakespeare has *forth* very often with the sense of *out* or *abroad*.

[66] *Blunt* here means, apparently, *dull* or *slow ;* alluding to the "tardy
form " Casca has just " put on " in winding so long about the matter before
coming to the point.—" He was quick mettle " means, He was of a *lively
spirit.   Mettlesome* is still used of spirited horses.   See page 46, note 6;
also, *Hamlet*, page 51, note 27.

However he puts on this tardy form.[67]
This rudeness is a sauce to his good wit,
Which gives men stomach to digest his words
With better appetite.

   Bru. And so it is. For this time I will leave you:
To-morrow, if you please to speak with me,
I will come home to you; or, if you will,
Come home to me, and I will wait for you.

   Cass. I will do so: till then, think of the world. —

                        [Exit BRUTUS.

Well, Brutus, thou art noble; yet, I see,
Thy honourable metal may be wrought
From that it is disposed:[68] therefore 'tis meet
That noble minds keep ever with their likes;
For who so firm that cannot be seduced?
Cæsar doth bear me hard,[69] but he loves Brutus:
If I were Brutus now, and he were Cassius,
He should not humour me.[70]   I will this night,

   [67] *However* for *although*, or *notwithstanding*. Often so.—" *Tardy* form "
is form of *tardiness*. So the Poet has *shady stealth* for *stealing shadow*, and
" *negligent* danger " for danger *from negligence*.

   [68] Wrought from *what*, or from that *which* it is disposed *to*. The Poet
has divers instances of prepositions thus omitted. — Of course Cassius is
here chuckling over the effect his talk has had upon Brutus. He evidently
regards Brutus as a noble putty-head, and goes on to take order for mould-
ing him accordingly.

   [69] The phrase to *bear one hard* occurs three times in this play, but nowhere else in Shakespeare. It seems to have been borrowed from horse-
manship, and to mean *carries a tight rein*, or *reins hard*, like one who *dis-
trusts* his horse. So before: "You bear too stubborn and too strange a
hand over your friend that loves you"; that is, "You hold me too hard on
the bit, like a strange rider, who is doubtful of his steed, and not like one
who confides in his faithful horse, and so rides him with an easy rein."—
For this note I am indebted to Mr. Joseph Crosby.

   [70] To *humour* a man, as the word is here used, is to turn and wind and
manage him by watching his moods and crotchets, and touching him ac-

In several hands,[71] in at his window throw,
As if they came from several citizens,
Writings all tending to the great opinion
That Rome holds of his name ;[72] wherein obscurely
Cæsar's ambition shall be glancèd at :
And, after this, let Cæsar seat him sure ;
For we will shake him, or worse days endure.[73]   [*Exit.*

SCENE III. — *The Same.   A Street.*

Thunder and Lightning.   Enter, from opposite sides, CASCA,
with his sword drawn, and CICERO.

Cic. Good even, Casca : brought you Cæsar home ?[1]
Why are you breathless ? and why stare you so ?

cordingly. It is somewhat in doubt whether the last *he* refers to Brutus or
to Cæsar. If to Brutus, the meaning of course is, " he should not play upon
my humours and fancies as I do upon his." And this sense is, I think,
fairly required by the context. For the whole speech is occupied with the
speaker's success in cajoling Brutus, and with plans for cajoling and shaping
him still further.

71 *Hands* for *handwritings*, of course. The Poet has it repeatedly so.

72 Now when Cassius felt his friends, and did stir them up against Cæsar,
they all agreed, and promised to take part with him, so Brutus were the
chief of their conspiracy. For they told him that so high an enterprise and
attempt as that did not so much require men of manhood and courage to
draw their swords, as it stood them upon to have a man of such estimation
as Brutus, to make every man boldly think that by his only presence the
fact were holy and just. — PLUTARCH.

73 " We will either shake him, or endure worse days in suffering the consequences of our attempt." — The Poet makes Cassius overflow with intense
personal spite against Cæsar. This is in accordance with what he read
in Plutarch : " Cassius, being a choleric man, and hating Cæsar privately
more than he did the tyranny openly, incensed Brutus against him. It is
also reported that Brutus could evil away with the tyranny, and that Cassius
hated the tyrant." Of course *tyranny* as here used means *royalty*.

1 To *bring* for to *escort* or *go along with* was very common.

Casca. Are not you moved, when all the sway of Earth
Shakes like a thing unfirm?[2] (O Cicero !
I have seen tempests, when the scolding winds
Have rived the knotty oaks ; and I have seen
Th' ambitious ocean swell and rage and foam,
To be exalted with the threatening clouds :[3]
But never till to-night, never till now,
Did I go through a tempest dropping fire.)
Either there is a civil strife in Heaven,
Or else the world, too saucy with the gods,
Incenses them to send destruction.[4]

　　Cic. Why, saw you any thing more wonderful?[5]

　　Casca. A common slave — you'd know him well by
　　　　sight[6] —
Held up his left hand, which did flame and burn
Like twenty torches join'd ; and yet his hand,
Not sensible[7] of fire, remain'd unscorch'd.
Besides, — I ha' not since put up my sword, —
Against the Capitol I met a lion,
Who glared upon me, and went surly by,
Without annoying me : and there were drawn
Upon a heap[8] a hundred ghastly women,

---

　[2] *Sway* for *constitution* or *order*, probably. In such a raging of the elements, it seems as if the whole world were going to pieces, or as if the Earth's steadfastness were growing *unfirm*, that is, *unsteady.*

　[3] *So as*, or *insomuch as* to be exalted with the threatening clouds. The Poet often uses the infinitive mood thus.

　[4] Either the gods are fighting among themselves, or else they are making war on the world for being too saucy with them.

　[5] *More* is here equivalent to *else :* " Saw you any thing more *that was* wonderful ? "

　[6] " You would *recognise* him as a common slave, from his looks."

　[7] *Sensible*, here, is *sensitive*, or having sensation. Repeatedly so.

　[8] " Drawn *upon a heap* " is drawn *together in a crowd.*

Transformèd with their fear ; who swore they saw
Men, all in fire, walk up and down the streets.
And yesterday the bird of night [9] did sit
Even at noon-day upon the market-place,
Hooting and shrieking.   When these prodigies
Do so conjointly meet,[10] let not men say,
These are their reasons ; they are natural; [11]

[9] The old Roman horror of this bird is well shown in a passage of Holland's Pliny, as quoted in the Clarendon edition : " The screechowl betokeneth always some heavy news, and is most execrable in the presages of public affairs.   In sum, he is the very monster of the night.   There fortuned one of them to enter the very sanctuary of the Capitol, in that year when Sextus Papellio Ister and Lucius Pedanius were Consuls; whereupon, at the Nones of March, the city of Rome that year made general processions, to appease the wrath of the gods, and was solemnly purged by sacrifices."

[10] Certainly destiny may easier be foreseen than avoided, considering the strange and wonderful signs that were said to be seen before Cæsar's death.   For, touching the fires in the element, and spirits running up and down in the night, and also the solitary birds to be seen at noondays sitting in the great market-place, are not all these signs perhaps worth the noting, in such a wonderful chance as happened ?   But Strabo the philosopher writeth, that divers men were seen going up and down in fire, and furthermore, that there was a slave of the soldiers that did cast a marvellous burning flame out of his hand, insomuch as they that saw it thought he had been burnt; but when the fire was out, it was found he had no hurt.   Cæsar self also, doing sacrifice unto the gods, found that one of the beasts which was sacrificed had no heart: and that was a strange thing in nature, how a beast could live without a heart. — PLUTARCH.

[11] The language is obscure, but the meaning probably is, " These things *have* their reasons ; they proceed from natural causes."   Casca refers to the doctrine of the Epicureans, who were slow to believe that such elemental pranks had any moral significance in them, or that moral causes had any thing to do with them ; and held that the reasons of them were to be sought for in the simple working of natural laws and forces.   The text has a good comment in *All's Well that Ends Well*, ii. 3 : " They say miracles are past ; and we have our philosophical persons, to make modern and familiar, things supernatural and causeless.   Hence it is that we make trifles of terrors ; ensconcing ourselves into seeming knowledge, when we should submit ourselves to an unknown fear."

For I believe they are portentous things
Unto the climate [12] that they point upon.

Cic. Indeed, it is a strange-disposèd time :
But men may construe things after their fashion,
Clean [13] from the purpose of the things themselves.
Comes Cæsar to the Capitol to-morrow?

Casca. He doth ; for he did bid Antonius
Send word to you he would be there to-morrow.

Cic. Good night, then, Casca : this disturbèd sky
Is not to walk in.

Casca.   Farewell, Cicero.   [*Exit* CICERO.

Enter CASSIUS.

Cass. Who's there?
Casca.   A Roman.
Cass.   Casca, by your voice.
Casca. Your ear is good.   Cassius, what night is this ! [14]
Cass. A very pleasing night to honest men.
Casca. Who ever knew the Heavens menace so?
Cass. Those that have known the Earth so full of faults.
For my part, I have walk'd about the streets,
Submitting me unto the perilous night ;
And, thus umbracèd, [15] Casca, as you see,
Have bared my bosom to the thunder-stone : [16]

---

[12] *Climate* for *region* or *country*.   In *Hamlet* we have *climature* with the same meaning.   Also " Christian *climate* " in *Richard the Second*, iv. 1.

[13] *Clean*, here, is *altogether*, *entirely*, or *quite*.   Repeatedly so.   See *Richard the Second*, page 97, note 2. — The mild scepticism of Cicero's speech is very graceful and apt.

[14] We should say, " What *a* night is this ! "   In such exclamative phrases, as also in some others, the Poet omits the article when his verse wants it so.

[15] *Unbuttoned*.   Shakespeare gives the Romans his own dressing-gear.

[16] *Thunder-stone* is the old word for *thunder-bolt*.

And when the cross [17] blue lightning seem'd to open
The breast of Heaven, I did present myself
Even in the aim and very flash of it.

    Casca. But wherefore did you so much tempt the Heavens?
It is the part of men to fear and tremble,
When the most mighty gods by tokens send
Such dreadful heralds to astonish us.

    Cass. You are dull, Casca; and those sparks of life
That should be in a Roman you do want,
Or else you use not. You look pale, and gaze,
And put on fear, and case yourself in wonder,[18]
To see the strange impatience of the Heavens:
But if you would consider the true cause
Why all these fires, why all these gliding ghosts,
Why birds and beasts, from quality and kind;[19]
Why old men fool, and children calculate;—
Why all these things change from their ordinance,
Their natures, and preformèd faculties,
To monstrous quality;[20]—why, you shall find

    [17] *Cross* for the *zigzag path* of lightning. So in *King Lear*, iv. 7: "Was this a face to stand in the most terrible and nimble stroke of quick, *cross* lightning?"

    [18] That is, *put on a look* or *expression* of wonder. So in *Much Ado*, iv. 1: "I am so *attired in wonder*, I know not what to say."

    [19] *Quality* is *office* or *calling*. Often so. *Kind* is *nature*. Also frequent. So in *Antony and Cleopatra*, last scene: "The worm will do his kind"; that is, will do as its *nature* is or prompts. The same in the old proverb, "The cat will after kind."—To make sense of the line, some word must be understood; probably *change*, from the second line below.

    [20] The grammar of this passage is rather confused, yet the meaning is clear enough; the general idea being that of elements and animals, and even of old men and children, acting in a manner out of or against their nature; or changing their natures and original faculties from the course, in which they were ordained to move, to monstrous or unnatural modes of action.

That Heaven hath infused them with these spirits,
To make them instruments of fear and warning
Unto some monstrous state.[21]   Now could I, Casca,
Name thee a man most like this dreadful night;
That thunders, lightens, opens graves, and roars,
As doth the lion, in the Capitol;[22]
A man no mightier than thyself or me
In personal action; yet prodigious grown,
And fearful, as these strange eruptions are.

 Casca. 'Tis Cæsar that you mean; is it not, Cassius?

 Cass. Let it be who it is:[23] for Romans now
Have thews[24] and limbs like to their ancestors;
But, woe the while! our fathers' minds are dead,
And we are govern'd with[25] our mothers' spirits;
Our yoke and sufferance show us womanish.

 Casca. Indeed, they say the Senators to-morrow
Mean to establish Cæsar as a king;
And he shall wear his crown by sea and land,
In every place, save here in Italy.

 Cass. I know where I will wear this dagger then;

---

[21] That is, some prodigious or abnormal condition of things. Elsewhere the Poet has "enormous state," with the same meaning. See *King Lear*, page 110, note 31. — As Cassius is an avowed Epicurean, it may seem out of character to make him speak thus. But he is here talking for effect, his aim being to kindle and instigate Casca into the conspiracy; and to this end he does not stick to say what he does not himself believe.

[22] This reads as if a lion were kept in the Capitol to roar for them. But the meaning is that Cæsar roars in the Capitol, like a lion. Perhaps Cassius has the idea of Cæsar's claiming or aspiring to be among men what the lion is among beasts.

[23] Meaning, probably, "no matter who it is"; as the Clarendon notes.

[24] *Thews* for *sinews* or *muscles*. Always so in Shakespeare.

[25] Present usage would say "governed *by*." But Shakespeare very often uses *with* to denote the agent of a passive verb. So afterwards in this play: "Here is himself, marr'd, as you see, *with* traitors."

Cassius from bondage will deliver Cassius :
Therein, ye gods, you make the weak most strong ;
Therein, ye gods, you tyrants do defeat :
Nor stony tower, nor walls of beaten brass,
Nor airless dungeon, nor strong links of iron,
Can be retentive to the strength of spirit ;[26]
But life, being weary of these worldly bars,
Never lacks power to dismiss itself.
If I know this, know all the world besides,
That part of tyranny that I do bear
I can shake off at pleasure.   [*Thunders still.*

    Casca.   So can I :
So every bondman in his own hand bears
The power to cancel his captivity.

    Cass. And why should Cæsar be a tyrant then ?
Poor man ! I know he would not be a wolf,
But that he sees the Romans are but sheep :
He were no lion, were not Romans hinds.
Those that with haste will make a mighty fire
Begin it with weak straws :[27] what trash is Rome,
What rubbish, and what offal, when it serves
For the base matter to illuminate
So vile a thing as Cæsar ![28]   But, O grief,
Where hast thou led me ? I perhaps speak this
Before a willing bondman : then I know

    26 Can *retain*, *hold in*, or *repress* man's energy of soul.

    27 The idea seems to be that, as men start a huge fire with worthless
straws or shavings, so Cæsar is using the degenerate Romans of the time,
to set the whole world a-blaze with his own glory. Cassius's enthusiastic
hatred of "the mightiest Julius" is irresistibly delightful. For "a good
hater" is the next best thing to a true friend ; and Cassius's honest gushing
malice is far better than Brutus's stabbing sentimentalism.

    28 To shed splendour upon him, or to make a light for him to shine by.

My answer must be made ;[29] but I am arm'd,
And dangers are to me indifferent.

    Casca. You speak to Casca ; and to such a man
That is no fleering tell-tale.[30]   Hold, my hand :
Be factious for redress of all these griefs ;[31]
And I will set this foot of mine as far
As who goes farthest.

    Cass.   There's a bargain made.
Now know you, Casca, I have moved already
Some certain of the noblest-minded Romans
To undergo[32] with me an enterprise
Of honourable-dangerous consequence ;
And I do know, by this,[33] they stay for me
In Pompey's porch : for now, this fearful night,
There is no stir or walking in the streets ;
And the complexion of the element

---

   [29] The meaning is, " Perhaps you will go and blab to Cæsar all I have said about him ; and then he will call me to account for it.   Very well ; go tell him ; and let him do his worst : I care not."

   [30] *Fleering* unites the two senses of *flattering* and *mocking*, and so is just the right epithet for a tell-tale, who flatters you into saying that of another which you ought not to say, and then mocks you by going to that other and telling what you have said. — The meaning of the next clause is, " Hold, *here is* my hand "; as men clasp hands in striking or sealing a bargain.

   [31] *Be factious* is, probably, *form a party* or *faction*. Or it may mean "Be active"; the literal meaning of *factious*. — Here, as often, *griefs* is put for *grievances ;* that which *causes* griefs.

   [32] *Undergo* for *undertake*. So in *2 Henry the Fourth*, i. 3 : " How able such a work to *undergo*." And in several other places.

   [33] *By this* for by this *time*. So in various instances. — Pompey's porch was a spacious adjunct to the huge theatre that Pompey had built in the Campus Martius, outside of the city proper ; and where, as Plutarch says, " was set up an image of Pompey, which the city had made and consecrated in honour of him." There it was, in fact, that the stabbing took place, though Shakespeare transfers this to the Capitol.

Is favour'd like [34] the work we have in hand,
Most bloody-fiery and most terrible.

    Casca. Stand close [35] awhile, for here comes one in haste.

    Cass. 'Tis Cinna; I do know him by his gait;
He is a friend. —

Enter CINNA.

                Cinna, where haste you so?

    Cin. To find out you. Who's that? Metellus Cimber?

    Cass. No, it is Casca; one incorporate [36]
To our attempt. Am I not stay'd for, Cinna?

    Cin. I'm glad on't. What a fearful night is this!
There's two or three of us have seen strange sights.

    Cass. Am I not stay'd for? tell me.

    Cin.   Yes,
You are. O, Cassius, if you could but win
The noble Brutus to our party, —

    Cass. Be you content. Good Cinna, take this paper,
And look you lay it in the prætor's chair,
Where Brutus may best find it; and throw this
In at his window; set this up with wax
Upon old Brutus' statue: all this done,
Repair to Pompey's porch, where you shall find us.
Is Decius Brutus and Trebonius there?

    Cin. All but Metellus Cimber; and he's gone

---

[34] Is *featured*, has the same *aspect* or *countenance*. Shakespeare often uses *favour* in this sense. In the Poet's time, it was much in fashion to use *element* for *sky*. We have a ludicrous instance of this from Falstaff, in 2 *Henry the Fourth*, iv. 3: "If you do not all show like gilt two-pences to me, and I, in the clear sky of fame, o'ershine you as much as the full Moon doth the cinders of the *element*, which show like pins' heads to her, believe not the word of a noble."

[35] *Close* is *secret* or *in concealment*. A frequent usage.

[36] *Incorporate* is *closely united*, like the several parts of the body.

To seek you at your house.   Well, I will hie,[37]
And so bestow these papers as you bade me.

   Cass. That done, repair to Pompey's theatre. —

[*Exit* CINNA.

Come, Casca, you and I will yet, ere day,
See Brutus at his house : three parts of him
Is [38] ours already ; and the man entire,
Upon the next encounter, yields him ours.

   Casca. O, he sits high in all the people's hearts !
And that which would appear offence in us,
His countenance, like richest alchemy,[39]
Will change to virtue and to worthiness.

   Cass. Him, and his worth, and our great need of him,
You have right well conceited.[40]   Let us go,
For it is after midnight ; and; ere day,
We will awake him, and be sure of him.   [*Exeunt.*

---

   [37] *Hie* is *hasten.*   So in *Hamlet,* i. 1: "Th' extravagant and erring spirit
hies to his confine."   And in many other places.

   [38] Such combinations as *parts* and *is* were not then bad grammar.

   [39] Alchemy is the old *ideal* art of turning base metals into gold.

   [40] *Conceited* is *conceived, understood,* or *apprehended.*

ACT II.

Scene I. — *Rome.* Brutus's *Orchard.*[1]

Enter Brutus.

Bru. What, Lucius, ho !—
I cannot, by the progress of the stars,
Give guess how near to day. — Lucius, I say !—
I would it were my fault to sleep so soundly. —
When, Lucius, when ![2] Awake, I say ! what, Lucius !

Enter Lucius.

Luc. Call'd you, my lord? ·
Bru. Get me a taper in my study, Lucius :
When it is lighted, come and call me here.
Luc. I will, my lord.   [*Exit.*
Bru. It must be by his death :[3] and, for my part,
I know no personal cause to spurn at him,
But for the general.[4] He would be crown'd :
How that might change his nature, there's the question :
It is the bright day that brings forth the adder ;[5]

---

[1] *Orchard* and *garden* were synonymous. In *Romeo and Juliet*, Capulet's *garden* is twice called *orchard*.

[2] *When!* was sometimes used as an exclamation of impatience.

[3] Brutus has been casting about on all sides to find some other means to prevent Cæsar's being king, and here gives it up that this can be done only by killing him. Thus the speech opens in just the right way to throw us back upon his antecedent meditations.

[4] The *public cause.* This use of *general* was common.

[5] The Poet is apt to be right in his observation of Nature. In a bright warm day the snakes come out to bask in the sun. And the idea is, that the sunshine of royalty will kindle the serpent in Cæsar.

And that craves wary walking.   Crown him? — that :
And then, I grant, we put a sting in him,
That at his will he may do danger with.[6]
Th' abuse of greatness is, when it disjoins
Remorse from power ; and, to speak truth of Cæsar,
I have not known when his affections sway'd
More than his reason.[7] But 'tis a common proof,[8]
That lowliness is young ambition's ladder,
Whereto the climber-upward turns his face ;
But, when he once attains the upmost round,
He then unto the ladder turns his back,
Looks in the clouds, scorning the base degrees [9]
By which he did ascend : so Cæsar may ;
Then, lest he may, prevent.   And, since the quarrel [10]
Will bear no colour for the thing he is,
Fashion it thus, — that what he is, augmented,

---

6 That is, do *mischief* with, and so *be* or *prove dangerous.*

7 Some obscurity here, owing to the use of certain words in uncommon senses. *Remorse,* in Shakespeare, commonly means *pity* or *compassion :* here it means *conscience,* or *conscientiousness.* So in *Othello,* iii. 3 : "Let him command, and to obey shall be in me *remorse,* what bloody work soe'er." The possession of dictatorial power is apt to stifle or sear the conscience, so as to make a man literally remorseless. *Affections,* again, here stands for *passions,* as in several other instances. Finally, *reason* is here used in the same sense as *remorse.* So the context clearly points out; and the conscience is, in a philosophical sense, the *moral* reason.

8 *Proof* for *fact,* or the thing *proved.* So in Bacon's essay *Of Parents and Children :* "The *proof* is best when men keep their authority towards their children, but not their purse"; where the meaning is, it *proves,* or *turns out,* best.

9 *Base degrees* is *lower steps ; degree* being used in its primitive sense, and for the rounds of the ladder. Elsewhere the Poet has *base* for *lower.* See *Richard II.,* page 115, note 17.

10 *Quarrel* for *cause.* So in the 35th Psalm of *The Psalter :* "Stand up to judge my *quarrel;* avenge Thou my *cause."* And Shakespeare has it repeatedly so. See *Macbeth,* page 141, note 23.

Would run to these and these extremities : [11]
And therefore think him as a serpent's egg,
Which, hatch'd, would, as his kind, grow mischievous ;
And kill him in the shell.

Re-enter LUCIUS.

Luc. The taper burneth in your closet, sir.
Searching the window for a flint, I found
This paper thus seal'd up ; and I am sure
It did not lie there when I went to bed.

Bru. Get you to bed again ; it is not day.
Is not to-morrow, boy, the Ides of March ?

Luc. I know not, sir.

Bru. Look in the calendar, and bring me word.

Luc. I will, sir.   [*Exit.*

Bru. The exhalations,[12] whizzing in the air,

---

[11] Something of obscurity again. But the meaning is, " Since we have
no *show* or *pretext* of a cause, no assignable or apparent ground of complaint, against Cæsar, in what he is, or in any thing he has yet done, let us
assume that the further addition of a crown will quite upset his nature, and
metamorphose him into a serpent." The strain of casuistry used in this
speech is very remarkable. Coleridge found it perplexing. Upon the sup-
posal that Shakespeare meant Brutus for a wise and good man, the speech
seems to me utterly unintelligible. But the Poet, I think, must have regarded him simply as a well-meaning, but conceited and shallow idealist ;
and such men are always cheating and puffing themselves with the thinnest
of sophisms ; feeding on air, and conceiving themselves inspired ; or, as
Gibbon puts it, " mistaking the giddiness of the head for the illumination of
the Spirit."

[12] *Exhalations* for *meteors*, or *meteoric lights ;* referring to the flashes of
lightning. In Plutarch's *Opinions of Philosophers*, as translated by Holland,
we have the following : " Aristotle supposeth that all these *meteors* come of
a dry *exhalation*, which, being gotten enclosed within a moist cloud, striveth
forcibly to get forth : now, by attrition and breaking together, it causeth the
clap of thunder." Shakespeare has *meteor* repeatedly in the same way. So
in *Romeo and Juliet*, iii. 5 : " It is some *meteor* that the Sun *exhales*."

Give so much light that I may read by them. —

                     [*Opens the paper, and reads.*

Brutus, thou sleep'st: awake and see thyself.

Shall Rome, &c.   Speak, strike, redress! —

Brutus, thou sleep'st: awake! —

Such instigations have been often dropp'd

Where I have took them up.[13]

Shall Rome, &c.   Thus must I piece it out:

Shall Rome stand under one man's awe?   What, Rome?

My ancestor did from the streets of Rome

The Tarquin drive, when he was call'd a king. —

Speak, strike, redress! — Am I entreated, then,

To speak and strike?   O Rome, I make thee promise,

If the redress will follow, thou receivest

Thy full petition at the hand of Brutus!

[13] Here the Poet had in his eye the following from Plutarch: "For Brutus, his friends and countrymen, both by divers procurements and sundry rumours of the city, and by many bills also, did openly call and procure him to do that he did. For, under the image of his ancestor Junius Brutus, that drave the kings out of Rome, they wrote, ' O, that it pleased the gods thou wert now alive, Brutus!' and again, 'That thou wert here among us now!' His tribunal or chair, where he gave audience during the time he was Prætor, was full of such bills: 'Brutus, thou art asleep, and art not Brutus indeed.'" — Mr. Philip Smith, in his *History of the World*, comments upon the matter as follows: "Brutus, having joined the Pompeian standard with reluctance, had been the first to submit after the battle of Pharsalia, and had been ever since distinguished by Cæsar's special favour. But hints which his patron was said to have dropped of Brutus's worthiness to fill his place aided the plausible appeals which his brother-in-law Cassius made to his vanity. The mind which could be caught by such tricks as placards hung upon the statue of the elder Brutus with the inscription, 'Would thou wert alive!' — by billets thrust into his own hands, bearing the words, 'Brutus, thou sleepest, thou art no Brutus!' — had as little of stern principle as the heart that could plant the last dagger in Cæsar's bosom had of gratitude." The same writer ascribes, and justly too, the concocting of the conspiracy to " a narrow selfish jealousy of Cæsar's ascendency."

Re-enter LUCIUS.

Luc. Sir, March is wasted fourteen days.

[*Knocking within.*

Bru. 'Tis good.   Go to the gate ; somebody knocks. —

[*Exit* LUCIUS.

Since Cassius first did whet me against Cæsar,
I have not slept.
Between the acting of a dreadful thing
And the first motion,[14] all the interim is
Like a phantasma[15] or a hideous dream :
The genius and the mortal instruments
Are then in council ;[16] and the state of man,

---

[14] *Motion* for *impulse*, or the first budding of thought into purpose.

[15] A *phantasma* is a *phantom;* something imagined or fancied; a vision of things that are not, as in a nightmare.

[16] Commentators differ about *genius* here; some taking it for the *con-science*, others for the *anti-conscience*. Shakespeare uses *genius, spirit,* and *demon* as synonymous, and all three, apparently, both in a good sense and in a bad; as every man was supposed to have a good and a bad angel. So, in this play, we have " thy *evil spirit*"; in *The Tempest,* " our *worser genius*"; in *Troilus and Cressida,* " Some say the *genius* so cries *Come!* to him that instantly must die "; in *Antony and Cleopatra,* " Thy *demon,* that's thy *spirit* which keeps thee "; where, as often, *keeps* is *guards.* In these and some other cases, the words have some epithet or context that determines their meaning ; but not so with *genius* in the text. But, in all such cases, the words, I think, mean the *directive* power of the mind. And so we often speak of a man's *better self,* or a man's *worser self,* according as one is in fact *directed* or *drawn* to good or to evil. — The sense of *mortal,* here, is also somewhat in question. The Poet sometimes uses it for *perishable,* or that which *dies;* but oftener for *deadly,* or that which *kills. Mortal instruments* may well be held to mean the same as when Macbeth says, " I'm settled, and bend up each *corporal agent* to this terrible feat." — As Brutus is speaking with reference to his own case, he probably intends *genius* in a good sense; for the spiritual or immortal part of himself. If so, then he would naturally mean, by *mortal,* his perishable part, or his *ministerial* faculties, which shrink from executing what the *directive* power is urging them to. —

Like to a little kingdom, suffers then
The nature of an insurrection.[17]

Re-enter LUCIUS.

Luc. Sir, 'tis your brother Cassius at the door,
Who doth desire to see you.
  Bru.   Is he alone?
  Luc. No, sir, there are more with him.
  Bru.   Do you know them?
  Luc. No, sir: their hats are pluck'd about their ears,
And half their faces buried in their cloaks,
That by no means I may discover them
By any mark of favour.
  Bru.   Let 'em enter. — [*Exit* LUCIUS.
They are the faction. — O conspiracy,
Shamest thou to show thy dangerous brow by night,
When evils are most free?[18] O, then, by day
Where wilt thou find a cavern dark enough
To mask thy monstrous visage? Seek none, conspiracy;
Hide it in smiles and affability:
For if thou pass, thy native semblance on,[19]
Not Erebus itself were dim enough
To hide thee from prevention.[20]

The late Professor Ferrier, however, of Aberdeen, seems to take a somewhat different view of the passage. "Shakespeare," says he, "has a fine description of the unsettled state of the mind when the will is hesitating about
the perpetration of a great crime, and when the passions are threatening to
overpower, and eventually do overpower, the reason and the conscience."

 [17] That is, a *kind* of insurrection, or *something like* an insurrection.

 [18] When *crimes* and *mischiefs*, or rather when evil and mischievous *men*
are most free from the restraints of law, or of shame. So Hamlet speaks of
night as the time "when Hell itself breathes out contagion to this world."

 [19] "Thy native semblance *being* on." Ablative absolute again.

 [20] "To hide thee from *discovery*," which would lead to prevention. — Of

Enter CASSIUS, CASCA, DECIUS, CINNA, METELLUS CIMBER, *and*
TREBONIUS.

   Cass. I think we are too bold upon your rest :
Good morrow, Brutus ; do we trouble you ?
   Bru. I have been up this hour, awake all night.
Know I these men that come along with you ?
   Cass. Yes, every man of them ; and no man here
But honours you ; and every one doth wish
You had but that opinion of yourself
Which every noble Roman bears of you.
This is Trebonius.
   Bru.   He is welcome hither.
   Cass. This Decius[21] Brutus.
   Bru.   He is welcome too.
   Cass. This, Casca ; this, Cinna ; and this Metellus Cimber.
   Bru. They are all welcome. —
What watchful cares do interpose themselves
Betwixt your eyes and night ?
   Cass. Shall I entreat a word ?

                  [BRUTUS *and* CASSIUS *whisper apart.*
   Dec. Here lies the East : doth not the day break here ?
   Casca. No.
   Cin. O, pardon, sir, it doth ; and yon gray lines

---

the five divisions of Hades, Erebus was, properly, the third. Shakespeare,
however, seems to identify it with Tartarus, the lowest deep of the infernal
world, the horrible pit where Dante locates Brutus and Cassius along with
Judas Iscariot.

21 Shakespeare found the name thus in Plutarch. In fact, however, it
was *Decimus*, not *Decius*. The man is said to have been cousin to the other
Brutus of the play. He had been one of Cæsar's ablest, most favoured, and
most trusted lieutenants, and had particularly distinguished himself in his
naval service at Venetia and Massilia. After the murder of Cæsar, he was
found to be written down in his will as second heir.

That fret the clouds are messengers of day.

   Casca. You shall confess that you are both deceived.
Here, as I point my sword, the Sun arises ;
Which is a great way growing on the South,
Weighing the youthful season of the year.[22]
Some two months hence, up higher toward the North
He first presents his fire ; and the high East
Stands, as the Capitol, directly here.[23]

   Bru. Give me your hands all over, one by one.

   Cass. And let us swear our resolution.

   Bru. No, not an oath : if not the face of men,[24]
The sufferance of our souls, the time's abuse, —
If these be motives weak, break off betimes,
And every man hence to his idle bed ;
So let high-sighted tyranny range on,
Till each man drop by lottery.[25] But if these,
As I am sure they do, bear fire enough
To kindle cowards, and to steel with valour
The melting spirits of women ; then, countrymen,

---

[22] That is, *verging* or *inclining towards* the South, *in accordance with* the early time of the year. *Weighing* is *considering*.

[23] "The *high* East " is the *perfect* East. So the Poet has " *high* morning' for morning *full-blown*. — This little side-talk on an indifferent theme is very finely conceived, and aptly marks the men as seeking to divert off the anxious thoughts of the moment by any casual chat. It also serves the double purpose of showing that they are not listening, and of preventing suspicion, if any were listening to them.

[24] Meaning, probably, the shame and self-reproach with which Romans must now *look each other in the face*, under the consciousness of having fallen away from the republican spirit of their forefathers. — The change in the construction of the sentence gives it a more colloquial cast, without causing any real obscurity.

[25] Brutus seems to have in mind the capriciousness of a high-looking and heaven-daring oriental tyranny, where men's lives hung upon the nod and whim of the tyrant, as on the hazards of a lottery.

What[26] need we any spur but our own cause
To prick us to redress? what other bond
Than secret Romans, that have spoke the word,
And will not palter?[27] and what other oath
Than honesty to honesty engaged,[28]
That this shall be, or we will fall for it?
Swear priests, and cowards, and men cautelous,[29]
Old feeble carrions,[30] and such suffering souls
That welcome wrongs; unto bad causes swear
Such creatures as men doubt: but do not stain
The even virtue[31] of our enterprise,
Nor th' insuppressive[32] mettle of our spirits,
To think that or our cause or[33] our performance
Did need an oath; when every drop of blood
That every Roman bears, and nobly bears,
Is guilty of a several bastardy,
If he do break the smallest particle
Of any promise that hath pass'd from him.

26 *What* for *why*. The Poet often has it so. And so in St. Mark, xiv. 63: "*What* need we any further witnesses?"

27 To *palter* is to *equivocate*, to *shuffle*, as in making a promise with what is called "a mental reservation."

28 *Engaged* is *pledged*, or *put in pawn*. A frequent usage.

29 *Cautelous* is here used in the sense of *deceit* or *fraud;* though its original meaning is *wary*, *circumspect*, the same as *cautious*. The word is said to have caught a bad sense in passing through French hands. But, as the Clarendon edition notes, "the transition from caution to suspicion, and from suspicion to craft and deceit, is not very abrupt."

30 *Carrions* for *carcasses*, or men as good as dead. Repeatedly so.

31 Meaning the virtue that holds an equable and uniform tenour, always keeping the same high level.

32 *Insuppressive* for *insuppressible;* the active form with the passive sense. So the Poet has *unexpressive* for *inexpressible*. See, also, *Hamlet*, page 77, note 9.

33 *Or* — *or* for *either* — *or* occurs very often in all English poetry; as also *nor* — *nor* for *neither* — *nor*. — *To think* is *by thinking*.

Cass. But what of Cicero? Shall we sound him?
I think he will stand very strong with us.

Casca. Let us not leave him out.

Cin.   No, by no means.

Met. O, let us have him ! for his silver hairs
Will purchase us a good opinion,[34]
And buy men's voices to commend our deeds :
It shall be said, his judgment ruled our hands ;
Our youths and wildness shall no whit appear,
But all be buried in his gravity.

Bru. O, name him not ! let us not break with him ;[35]
For he will never follow any thing
That other men begin.

Cass.   Then leave him out.

Casca. Indeed, he is not fit.

Dec. Shall no man else be touch'd but only Cæsar?

Cass. Decius, well urged. — I think it is not meet,
Mark Antony, so well beloved of Cæsar,
Should outlive Cæsar : we shall find of him[36]
A shrewd contriver ; and you know, his means,
If he improve them, may well stretch so far
As to annoy us all : which to prevent,
Let Antony and Cæsar fall together.

[34] *Opinion* for *reputation* or *estimation.* Often so. Observe the thread of association in *silver, purchase,* and *buy.*

[35] Old language for " let us not break *the matter to* him." — This bit of dialogue is very charming. Brutus knows full well that Cicero is not the man to play second fiddle to any of *them ;* that if he have any thing to do with the enterprise it must be as the leader of it ; and that is just what Brutus wants to be himself. Merivale thinks it a great honour to Cicero, that the conspirators did not venture to propose the matter to him.

[36] We should say "find *in* him." So in *The Merchant,* iii. 5 : "Even such a husband hast thou *of* me as she is for a wife."

Bru. Our course will seem too bloody, Caius Cassius,
To cut the head off, and then hack the limbs,
Like wrath in death, and envy[37] afterwards;
For Antony is but a limb of Cæsar.
Let us be sacrificers, but not butchers, Caius.
We all stand up against the spirit of Cæsar;
And in the spirit of men there is no blood:
O, that we then could come by Cæsar's spirit,
And not dismember Cæsar! But, alas,
Cæsar must bleed for it! And, gentle friends,
Let's kill him boldly, but not wrathfully;
Let's carve him as a dish fit for the gods,
Not hew him as a carcass fit for hounds:
And let our hearts, as subtle masters do,
Stir up their servants to an act of rage,
And after seem to chide 'em.[38] This shall mark
Our purpose necessary,[39] and not envious;
Which so appearing to the common eyes,
We shall be call'd purgers,[40] not murderers.

[37] Here, as commonly in Shakespeare, *envy* is *malice* or *hatred*. And so, a little after, *envious* is *malicious*. — North's Plutarch gives the matter of this passage as follows: "They consulted whether they should kill Antonius with Cæsar. But Brutus would in no wise consent to it, saying that, venturing on such an enterprise as that, for the maintenance of law and justice, it ought to be clear from all villainy. Yet they, fearing Antonius's power, and the authority of his office, appointed certain of the conspiracy, that when Cæsar were gone into the Senate, and while others should execute their enterprise, they should keep Antonius in a talk out of the Senate-house."

[38] So the King proceeds with Hubert in *King John*. And so men often proceed when they wish to have a thing done, and to shirk the responsibility; setting it on by dark hints and allusions, and then, after it is done, affecting to blame or to scold the doers of it.

[39] That is, "*will* mark our purpose *as* necessary," or the offspring of necessity. The indiscriminate use of *shall* and *will* is frequent.

[40] Meaning *healers*, who cleanse the land from the disease of tyranny.

And for Mark Antony, think not of him ;
For he can do no more than Cæsar's arm
When Cæsar's head is off.

    Cass.   Yet I do fear him ;
For in th' ingrafted love he bears to Cæsar —

    Bru. Alas, good Cassius, do not think of him :
If he love Cæsar, all that he can do
Is to himself, — take thought and die [41] for Cæsar :
And that were much he should ; for he is given
To sports, to wildness, and much company.

    Treb. There is no fear in him ; [42] let him not die ;
For he will live, and laugh at this hereafter.   [*Clock strikes.*

    Bru. Peace ! count the clock.

    Cass.   The clock hath stricken three.

    Treb. 'Tis time to part.

    Cass.   But it is doubtful yet
Whêr Cæsar will come forth to-day or no ;
For he is superstitious grown of late,
Quite from the main [43] opinion he held once
Of fantasy, of dreams, and ceremonies. [44]

---

[41] " Think and die," or "take thought and die," is an old phrase for *grieve one's self to death :* and it would be much indeed, a very wonderful thing, if Antony should fall into any killing sorrow, such a light-hearted, jolly companion as he is. So the Poet uses *think* and *thought* repeatedly. And so in the Scripture phrases, "take no thought for your life," and " take no thought for the morrow," the Greek word translated *take thought* properly means to *be anxious* or *solicitous.*

[42] No fear *on account of* him, or *because of* him, is the meaning. So *in* is used in several other places. See *Macbeth,* page 99, note 7.

[43] *Great, strong, mighty* are among the old senses of *main.* And *from,* in Shakespeare, often has the force of *contrary to.* So in Hamlet's saying, " is *from* the purpose of playing."

[44] Cæsar was, in his philosophy, an Epicurean, as most of the educated Romans then also were. Hence he was, in opinion, strongly sceptical about dreams and ceremonial auguries. Nevertheless, as is apt to be the case

It may be, these apparent[45] prodigies.
The unaccustom'd terror of this night,
And the persuasion of his augurers,
May hold him from the Capitol to-day.

    Dec. Never fear that : if he be so resolved,
I can o'ersway him ; for he loves to hear
That unicorns may be betray'd with trees,
And bears with glasses, elephants with holes,
Lions with toils,[46] and men with flatterers :
But, when I tell him he hates flatterers,
He says he does, being then most flatteréd.
Let me work ;
For I can give his humour the true bent,
And I will bring him to the Capitol.

    Cass. Nay, we will all of us be there to fetch him.

    Bru. By the eighth hour : is that the uttermost ?

    Cin. Be that the uttermost ; and fail not then.

    Met. Caius Ligarius doth bear Cæsar hard,
Who rated him for speaking well of Pompey :
I wonder none of you have thought of him.

    Bru. Now, good Metellus, go along by him :[47]

---

with sceptics and freethinkers, his conduct, especially in his later years, was
marked with many gross instances of superstitious practice.

    [45] *Apparent,* here, is *evident* or *manifest.* A frequent usage.

    [46] The way to catch that fabulous old beast, the unicorn, is, to stand be-
fore a tree, and, when he runs at you, to slip aside, and let him stick his horn
into the tree : then you have him. See *The Faerie Queene,* ii. 5, 10. —
Bears are said to have been caught by putting looking-glasses in their way,
they being so taken with the images of themselves, that the hunters could
easily master them. — Elephants were beguiled into pitfalls, lightly covered
over with hurdles and turf ; a bait being placed thereon, to tempt them. —
Toil is *trap* or *snare.* So in *Antony and Cleopatra,* v. 2 : " As she would
catch another Antony in her strong *toil* of grace."

    [47] That is, by his house : " make that your way home."

He loves me well, and I have given him reason ; [48]
Send him but hither, and I'll fashion him.

    Cass. The morning comes upon's : we'll leave you, Bru-
        tus : —
And, friends, disperse yourselves ; but all remember
What you have said, and show yourselves true Romans.

    Bru. Good gentlemen, look fresh and merrily ;
Let not our looks put on our purposes ; [49]
But bear it as our Roman actors do,
With untired spirits and formal constancy :
And so, good-morrow to you every one. —

                       [Exeunt all but BRUTUS.

Boy ! Lucius ! — Fast asleep?   It is no matter ;
Enjoy the honey-heavy dew of slumber : [50]
Thou hast no figures nor no fantasies,
Which busy care draws in the brains of men ;
Therefore thou sleep'st so sound.

               Enter PORTIA.

    Por.   Brutus, my lord !

    Bru. Portia, what mean you? wherefore rise you now?
It is not for your health thus to commit
Your weak condition to the raw-cold morning.

    Por. Nor for yours neither.   You've ungently, Brutus,

---

    [48] The meaning probably is, " given him reason to love me."

    [49] " Let not our looks betray our purposes by wearing, or being attired
with, any indication of them."

    [50] The compound epithet *honey-heavy* is very expressive and apt. The
" dew of slumber " is called *heavy* because it makes the subject feel heavy,
and *honey*-heavy because the heaviness it induces is sweet. — Brutus is naturally led to contrast the free and easy state of the boy's mind with that of
his own, which the excitement of his present undertaking is drawing full of
visions and images of trouble.

Stole from my bed : and yesternight, at supper,
You suddenly arose, and walk'd about,
Musing and sighing, with your arms across ;
And, when I ask'd you what the matter was,
You stared upon me with ungentle looks :
I urged you further ; then you scratch'd your head,
And too impatiently stamp'd with your foot :
Yet I insisted, yet you answer'd not ;
But, with an angry wafture of your hand,
Gave sign for me to leave you.   So I did ;
Fearing to strengthen that impatience
Which seem'd too much enkindled ; and withal
Hoping it was but an effect of humour,
Which sometime hath his hour with every man
It will not let you eat, nor talk, nor sleep ;
And, could it work so much upon your shape
As it hath much prevail'd on your condition,[51]
I should not know you, Brutus.   Dear my lord,
Make me acquainted with your cause of grief.

 Bru. I am not well in health, and that is all.

 Por. Brutus is wise, and, were he not in health,
He would embrace the means to come by it.

 Bru. Why, so I do.   Good Portia, go to bed.

 Por. Is Brutus sick ? and is it physical[52]
To walk unbracèd, and suck up the humours
Of the dank morning ?   What, is Brutus sick,
And will he steal out of his wholesome bed,
To dare the vile contagion of the night,

---

[51] *Condition* was much used for *temper* or *disposition*.   The term *ill-con-ditioned* is still in use for a cross-grained, irascible, or quarrelsome dispo-sition, or an ugly temper.

[52] The Poet has *physical* again for *wholesome* or *medicinal*, in *Coriolanus*, l. 5 : " The blood I drop is rather *physical* than dangerous to me."

And tempt the rheumy [53] and unpurgèd air
To add unto his sickness?   No, my Brutus;
You have some sick offence within your mind,
Which, by the right and virtue of my place,
I ought to know of: and, upon my knees,
I charge you, by my once-commended beauty,
By all your vows of love, and that great vow
Which did incorporate and make us one,
That you unfold to me, yourself, your half,
Why you are heavy, and what men to-night
Have had resort to you; for here have been
Some six or seven, who did hide their faces
Even from darkness.

    Bru.   Kneel not, gentle Portia.

    Por. I should not need, if you were gentle Brutus.
Within the bond of marriage, tell me, Brutus,
Is it excepted I should know no secrets
That appertain to you?   Am I yourself
But, as it were, in sort or limitation, —
To keep with you at meals, comfort your bed,
And talk to you sometimes?   Dwell I but in the suburbs
Of your good pleasure? [54]   If it be no more,
Portia is Brutus' harlot, not his wife.

    Bru. You are my true and honourable wife;
As dear to me as are the ruddy drops

---

[53] *Rheum* was specially used of the fluids that issue from the eyes or mouth. So in *Hamlet* we have "bisson *rheum*" for blinding *tears*. *Rheumy* here means that state of the air which causes the unhealthy issue of such fluids, or perhaps which makes people *rheumatic*. So, in *A Midsummer-Night's Dream*, ii. 1, Titania speaks of the Moon as "washing all the air, that rheumatic diseases do abound."

[54] In the outskirts or borders, and not at the centre or near the heart. The image is exceedingly apposite and expressive.

That visit my sad heart.[55]

   Por. If this were true, then should I know this secret.
I grant I am a woman ; but withal
A woman that Lord Brutus took to wife :
I grant I am a woman ; but withal
A woman well-reputed, Cato's daughter.
Think you I am no stronger than my sex,
Being so father'd and so husbanded ?
Tell me your counsels, I will not disclose 'em.
I have made strong proof of my constancy,
Giving myself a voluntary wound
Here in the thigh : can I bear that with patience,
And not my husband's secrets ?

   Bru.   O ye gods,
Render me worthy of this noble wife ![56] —[*Knocking within.*

---

[55] This embodies what was then known touching the circulation of the blood. William Harvey was born in 1578, fourteen years after Shakespeare, and his discovery was not published till 1628, twelve years after the Poet's death. The general fact of the circulation of the blood was known in ancient times ; and Harvey's discovery lay in ascertaining the *modus operandi* of it, and in reducing it to matter of strict science.

[56] Because she would not ask her husband what he ailed before she had made some proof by her self, she took a little razor, such as barbers occupy to pare men's nails, and, causing her maids and women to go out of her chamber, gave herself a great gash withal in her thigh, that she was straight all of a gore blood ; and incontinently after a vehement fever took her, by reason of the pain of her wound. Then, perceiving her husband was marvellously out of quiet, and that he could take no rest, even in her greatest pain of all she spake in this sort unto him : " I being, O Brutus, the daughter of Cato was married unto thee, not to be thy companion in bed and at board only, like a harlot, but to be partaker also with thee of thy good and evil fortune. Now, for thyself, I can find no cause of fault in thee, touching our match. But, for my part, how may I show my duty towards thee, and how much I would do for thy sake, if I cannot constantly bear a secret mischance or grief with thee, which requireth secresy and fidelity ? I confess that a woman's wit commonly is too weak to keep a secret safely ; but yet

Hark, hark ! one knocks : Portia, go in awhile ;
And by-and-by thy bosom shall partake
The secrets of my heart :
All my engagements I will construe to thee,
All the charáctery of my sad brows : [57]
Leave me with haste. [*Exit* PORTIA.] — Lucius, who's that
       knocks ?

Cred.

Re-enter LUCIUS *with* LIGARIUS.

*Get Cæsar to
and inflict
him in
conversation
and stab him*

Luc. Here is a sick man that would speak with you.
Bru. Caius Ligarius, that Metellus spake of. —
Boy, stand aside. — Caius Ligarius, — how !
Lig. Vouchsafe good-morrow from a feeble tongue.
Bru. O, what a time have you chose out, brave Caius,
To wear a kerchief ! [58] Would you were not sick !
Lig. I am not sick, if Brutus have in hand
Any exploit worthy the name of honour.

Brutus, good education and the company of virtuous men have some power
to reform the defect of nature. And, for myself, I have this benefit, moreover, that I am the daughter of Cato and wife of Brutus. This notwithstanding, I did not trust to any of these things before, until that now I have
found by experience, that no pain or grief whatsoever can overcome me."
With those words she showed him her wound on her thigh, and told him
what she had done to prove herself. Brutus was amazed to hear what she
said unto him ; and, lifting up his hands to heaven, he besought the gods to
give him the grace he might bring his enterprise to so good pass, that he
might be found a husband worthy of so noble a wife as Portia. So he then
did comfort her the best he could. — PLUTARCH.

[57] *Charáctery* is defined "writing by characters or strange marks." Brutus therefore means that he will divulge to her the secret cause of the sadness marked on his countenance.

[58] It was a common practice in England for those who were sick to wear
a kerchief on their heads. So in Fuller's *Worthies of Cheshire :* " If any
there be sick, they make him a posset and *tye a kerchief on his head ;* and if
that will not mend him, then God be merciful to him."

Bru. Such an exploit have I in hand, Ligarius,
Had you a healthful ear to hear of it.

Lig. By all the gods that Romans bow before,
I here discard my sickness.   Soul of Rome !
Brave son, derived from honourable loins !
Thou, like an exorcist,[59] hast conjured up
My mortified spirit.[60]   Now bid me run,
And I will strive with things impossible ;
Yea, get the better of them.[61]   What's to do?

Bru. A piece of work that will make sick men whole.

Lig. But are not some whole that we must make sick?

Bru. That must we also.   What it is, my Caius,
I shall unfold to thee, as we are going,
To whom it must be done.

Lig.   Set on your foot ;
And with a heart new-fired I follow you,
To do I know not what : but it sufficeth
That Brutus leads me on.

Bru.   Follow me, then.   [*Exeunt.*

[59] In Shakespeare's time, *exorcist* and *conjurer* were used indifferently.
The former has since come to mean only one who drives away spirits; the
latter, one who calls them up.

[60] That is, " my spirit which was dead in me."   Such is the literal meaning of *mortified ;* and so the Poet has it repeatedly.

[61] Amongst Pompey's friends, there was one called Caius Ligarius, who
had been accused unto Cæsar for taking part with Pompey, and Cæsar dis-
charged him.   But Ligarius thanked not Cæsar so much for his discharge,
as he was offended with him for that he was brought in danger by his
tyrannical power : and therefore in his heart he was always his mortal
enemy, and was besides very familiar with Brutus, who went to see him being
sick in his bed, and said unto him : " Ligarius, in what a time art thou sick ? "
Ligarius, rising up in his bed, and taking him by the right hand, said unto
him : " Brutus, if thou hast any great enterprise in hand, worthy of thyself,
I am whole." — PLUTARCH.

SCENE II. — *A Room in* CÆSAR'S *Palace.*

Thunder and Lightning. Enter CÆSAR, *in his night-gown.*

Cæs. Nor Heaven nor Earth have been at peace to-night :
Thrice hath Calpurnia in her sleep cried out,
Help, ho! they murder Cæsar! — Who's within?

Enter a Servant.

Serv. My lord?
Cæs. Go bid the priests do present sacrifice,
And bring me their opinions of success.[1]
Serv. I will, my lord.   [*Exit.*

Enter CALPURNIA.

Cal. What mean you, Cæsar? think you to walk forth?
You shall not stir out of your house to-day.
Cæs. Cæsar shall forth : the things that threaten me
Ne'er look but on my back ; when they shall see
The face of Cæsar, they are vanishéd.
Cal. Cæsar, I never stood on ceremonies,[2]
Yet now they fright me.   There is one within,
Besides the things that we have heard and seen,
Recounts most horrid sights seen by the watch.
A lioness hath whelpéd in the streets ;
And graves have yawn'd, and yielded up their dead ;
Fierce fiery warriors fought upon the clouds,
In ranks and squadrons and right form of war,
Which drizzled blood upon the Capitol ;

---

[1] Their opinions of what is to *follow*. The Poet often uses *success* in this
sense : so that we have "*good* success" and "*ill* success."

[2] *Ceremonies* is here put for the ceremonial or sacerdotal interpretation
of prodigies and omens.

The noise of battle hurtled[3] in the air;
Horses did neigh, and dying men did groan;
And ghosts did shriek and squeal about the streets.
O Cæsar, these things are beyond all use,
And I do fear them!

    Cæs.   What can be avoided
Whose end is purposed by the mighty gods?
Yet Cæsar shall go forth; for these predictions
Are to the world in general as to Cæsar.

    Cal. When beggars die, there are no comets seen;
The heavens themselves blaze forth the death of princes.

    Cæs. Cowards die many times before their deaths;
The valiant never taste of death but once.[4]
Of all the wonders that I yet have heard,
It seems to me most strange that men should fear;
Seeing that death, a necessary end,
Will come when it will come. —

Re-enter the Servant.

                    What say the augurers?

    Serv. They would not have you to stir forth to-day.
Plucking the entrails of an offering forth,
They could not find a heart within the beast.

    Cæs. The gods do this in shame of cowardice:

---

    [3] To *hurtle* is to clash, or move with violence and noise.

    [4] Plutarch relates that, a short time before Cæsar fell, some of his friends urged him to have a guard about him, and he replied that it was better to die at once than live in the continual fear of death. He is also said to have given as his reason for refusing a guard, that he thought Rome had more need of him than he of Rome; which was indeed true. And it is further stated that, on the eve of the fatal day, Cæsar being at the house of Lepidus with some friends, and the question being raised, "What kind of death is best?" he cut short the discussion by saying, "That which is least expected."

Cæsar should be a beast without a heart,
If he should stay at home to-day for fear.
No, Cæsar shall not : danger knows full well
That Cæsar is more dangerous than he :
We are two lions litter'd in one day,
And I the elder and more terrible ;
And Cæsar shall go forth.

 Cal.   Alas, my lord,
Your wisdom is consumed in confidence !
Do not go forth to-day : call it my fear
That keeps you in the house, and not your own,
We'll send Mark Antony to the Senate-house ;
And he shall say you are not well to-day :
Let me, upon my knee, prevail in this.

 Cæs. Mark Antony shall say I am not well ,
And, for thy humour, I will stay at home.[5]

Enter DECIUS.

Here's Decius Brutus, he shall tell them so.

[5] Then going to bed the same night, as his manner was, and lying with his wife Calpurnia, all the windows and doors of his chamber flying open, the noise awoke him, and made him afraid when he saw such light; but more, when he heard his wife Calpurnia, being fast asleep, weep and sigh, and put forth many fumbling lamentable speeches : for she dreamed that Cæsar was slain, and that she had him in her arms. Cæsar rising in the morning, she prayed him, if it were possible, not to go out of the doors that day, but to adjourn the session of the Senate until another day. And if that he made no reckoning of her dream, yet that he would search further of the soothsayers by their sacrifices, to know what should happen him that day. Thereby it seemed that Cæsar did likewise fear or suspect somewhat, because his wife Calpurnia until that time was never given to any fear and superstition; and that then he saw her so troubled in mind with this dream she had. But much more afterwards, when the soothsayers having sacrificed many beasts one after another, told him that none did like them : then he determined to send Antonius to adjourn the session of the Senate.—
PLUTARCH.

Dec. Cæsar, all hail! ·Good morrow, worthy Cæsar:
I come to fetch you to the Senate-house.

Cæs. And you are come in very happy time
To bear my greeting to the Senators,
And tell them that I will not come to-day.
Cannot, is false; and that I dare not, falser:
I will not come to-day. Tell them so, Decius.

Cal. Say he is sick.

Cæs.   Shall Cæsar send a lie?
Have I in conquest stretch'd mine arm so far,
To be afeard to tell gray-beards the truth?—
Decius, go tell them Cæsar will not come.

Dec. Most mighty Cæsar, let me know some cause,
Lest I be laugh'd at when I tell them so.

Cæs. The cause is in my will; I will not come:
That is enough to satisfy the Senate.
But, for your private satisfaction,
Because I love you, I will let you know:
Calpurnia here, my wife, stays me at home:
She dreamt to-night she saw my statua,[6]
Which, like a fountain with an hundred spouts,
Did run pure blood; and many lusty Romans
Came smiling, and did bathe their hands in it:
And these doth she apply for warnings and porténts
Of evils imminent; and on her knee
Hath begg'd that I will stay at home to-day.

Dec. This dream is all amiss interpreted :
It was a vision fair and fortunate.

[6] In Shakespeare's time *statue* was pronounced indifferently as a word
of two syllables or three. Bacon uses it repeatedly as a trisyllable, and spells
it *statua*, as in his *Advancement of Learning:* "It is not possible to have
the true pictures or *statuas* of Cyrus, Alexander, Cæsar, no, nor of the kings
or great personages of much later years."

Your statue spouting blood in many pipes,
In which so many smiling Romans bathed,
Signifies that from you great Rome shall suck
Reviving blood; and that great men shall press
For tinctures, stains, relics, and cognizance.[7]
This by Calpurnia's dream is signified.

   Cæs. And this way have you well expounded it.

   Dec. I have, when you have heard what I can say;
And know it now: The Senate have concluded
To give this day a crown to mighty Cæsar.[8]
If you shall send them word you will not come,
Their minds may change. Besides, it were a mock
Apt to be render'd,[9] for some one to say,
Break up the Senate till another time,
When Cæsar's wife shall meet with better dreams.
If Cæsar hide himself, shall they not whisper,
Lo, Cæsar is afraid?

[7] *Cognizance* is here used in a heraldic sense, as meaning any badge or token to show whose friends or servants the owners or wearers were. In ancient times, when martyrs or other distinguished men were executed, their friends often *pressed* to stain handkerchiefs with their blood, or to get some other relic, which they might keep, either as precious memorials of them, or as having a kind of sacramental virtue.

[8] The Roman people were specially yearning to avenge the slaughter of Marcus Crassus and his army by the Parthians; and Cæsar was at this time preparing an expedition against them. But a Sibylline oracle was alleged, that Parthia could only be conquered by a king; and it was proposed to invest Cæsar with the royal title and authority over the foreign subjects of the State. It is agreed on all hands that, if his enemies did not originate this proposal, they at least craftily urged it on, in order to make him odious, and exasperate the people against him. To the same end, they had for some time been plying the arts of extreme sycophancy, heaping upon him all possible honours, human and divine, hoping thereby to kindle such a fire of envy as would consume him.

[9] It were apt, or likely, to be *construed* or *represented* as a piece of mockery. So the Poet repeatedly uses the verb to *render*.

Pardon me, Cæsar; for my dear dear love
To your proceeding bids me tell you this;
And reason to my love is liable.[10]

　　Cæs. How foolish do your fears seem now, Calpurnia!
I am ashamèd I did yield to them.
Give me my robe, for I will go.[11]

Enter PUBLIUS, BRUTUS, LIGARIUS, METELLUS, CASCA, TRE-
BONIUS, *and* CINNA.

And look where Publius[12] is come to fetch me.
　　Pub. Good morrow, Cæsar.
　　Cæs. 　　　　　　　　Welcome, Publius. —
What, Brutus, are you stirr'd so early too? —
Good morrow, Casca. — Caius Ligarius,

---

[10] The thought here is, that love stands as principal, reason as second or
subordinate. "The deference which reason holds due from me to you is in
this instance *subject* and *amenable* to the calls of personal affection."

[11] In the mean time Decius Brutus, surnamed Albinus, in whom Cæsar
put such confidence, that in his last will and testament he had appointed him
to be his next heir, and yet was of the conspiracy with Cassius and Brutus;
he, fearing that, if Cæsar did adjourn the session that day, the conspiracy
would be betrayed, laughed at the soothsayers, and reproved Cæsar, saying
that "he gave the Senate occasion to mislike with him, and they might think
he mocked them, considering that by his commandment they were assembled, and that they were ready willingly to grant him all things, and to proclaim him king of all his provinces of the Empire of Rome out of Italy, and
that he should wear his diadem in all other places both by sea and land.
And furthermore, that if any man should tell them from him they should
depart for that present time, and return again when Calpurnia should have
better dreams, what would his enemies and ill-willers say, and how could
they like of his friends' words? And who could persuade them otherwise,
but that they should think his dominion a slavery unto them and tyrannical
in himself? And yet if it be so," said he, "that you utterly mislike of this
day, it is better that you go yourself in person, and, saluting the Senate, to
dismiss them till another time." Therewithal he took Cæsar by the hand,
and brought him out of his house. — PLUTARCH.

[12] This was Publius Silicius; not one of the conspirators.

Cæsar was ne'er so much your enemy
As that same ague which hath made you lean.[13] —
What is't o'clock?

Bru.   Cæsar, 'tis strucken eight.

Cæs. I thank you for your pains and courtesy.

Enter ANTONY.

See! Antony, that revels long o'nights,
Is notwithstanding up. — Good morrow, Antony.

Ant. So to most noble Cæsar.

Cæs.   Bid them prepare within:
I am to blame to be thus waited for. —
Now, Cinna; — now, Metellus; — what, Trebonius!
I have an hour's talk in store for you:
Remember that you call on me to-day;
Be near me, that I may remember you.

Treb. Cæsar, I will; — [*Aside.*] and so near will I be,
That your best friends shall wish I had been further.

Cæs. Good friends, go in, and taste some wine with me;
And we, like friends, will straightway go together.

Bru. [*Aside.*] That every like is not the same, O Cæsar,
The heart of Brutus yearns to think upon![14]   [*Exeunt.*

[13] Here, for the first time, we have Cæsar speaking fairly in character; for he was probably the most finished gentleman of his time, one of the sweetest of men, and as full of kindness as of wisdom and courage. Merivale aptly styles him " Cæsar the politic and the merciful."

[14] The winning and *honest* suavity of Cæsar here starts a pang of remorse in Brutus. Drinking wine together was regarded as a sacred pledge of truth and honour. Brutus knows that Cæsar is doing it in good faith; and it hurts him to think that the others *seem* to be doing the *like*, and yet are doing a very different thing. To *yearn* is to *grieve*, to *be pained*. Repeatedly used so by the Poet.

SCENE III. — *A Street near the Capitol.*

Enter ARTEMIDORUS, *reading a paper.*

Artem. *Cæsar, beware of Brutus; take heed of Cassius;
come not near Casca; have an eye to Cinna; trust not
Trebonius; mark well Metellus Cimber; Decius Brutus
loves thee not; thou hast wrong'd Caius Ligarius. There
is but one mind in all these men, and it is bent against
Cæsar. If thou be'st not immortal, look about you: security
gives way to conspiracy.[1] The mighty gods defend thee!*
                              Thy lover,   ARTEMIDORUS.

Here will I stand till Cæsar pass along,
And as a suitor will I give him this.
My heart laments that virtue cannot live
Out of the teeth of emulation.[2] —
If thou read this, O Cæsar, thou mayst live;
If not, the Fates with traitors do contrive.   [*Exit.*

SCENE IV. — *Another part of the same Street, before the
House of* BRUTUS.

Enter PORTIA *and* LUCIUS.

Por. I pr'ythee, boy, run to the Senate-house:
Stay not to answer me, but get thee gone.
Why dost thou stay?
     Luc.   To know my errand, madam.

---

[1] *Negligence* or *over-confidence makes* or *opens* a way for conspiracy. The
use of *security* and *secure* in this sense is very frequent. See *Hamlet*, page
83, note 8; also *Macbeth*, page 119, note 4.
[2] *Emulation* is *factious* and *envious rivalry.* So in *Troilus and Cressida*,
i. 3: "An *envious* fever of pale and bloodless *emulation.*"

Por. I would have had thee there, and here again,
Ere I can tell thee what thou shouldst do there. —
[*Aside.*] O constancy, be strong upon my side !
Set a huge mountain 'tween my heart and tongue !
I have a man's mind, but a woman's might.
How hard it is for women to keep counsel ! —
Art thou here yet?

    Luc.   Madam, what should I do?
Run to the Capitol, and nothing else?
And so return to you, and nothing else?

    Por. Yes ; bring me word, boy, if thy lord look well,
For he went sickly forth : and take good note
What Cæsar doth, what suitors press to him.
Hark, boy ! what noise is that?

    Luc. I hear none, madam.

    Por.   Pr'ythee, listen well :
I heard a bustling rumour,[3] like a fray,
And the wind brings it from the Capitol.

    Luc. Sooth,[4] madam, I hear nothing.

Enter ARTEMIDORUS.

    Por. Come hither, fellow : which way hast thou been?

    Artem. At mine own house, good lady.

    Por. What is't o'clock?

    Artem. About the ninth hour, lady.

    Por. Is Cæsar yet gone to the Capitol?

---

[3] A *loud noise* or *murmur*, as of stir and tumult, is one of the old meanings of *rumour.* — Since the interview of Brutus and Portia, he has unbosomed all his secrets to her ; and now she is in such a fever of anxiety, that she mistakes her own fancies for facts.

[4] *Sooth* for *in sooth ;* that is, *in truth*, or *truly.* A *soothsayer* is, properly, a *truth-speaker.* So the Poet often uses *sooth.*

Artem. Madam, not yet : I go to take my stand,
To see him pass on to the Capitol.

Por. Thou hast some suit to Cæsar, hast thou not?

Artem. That I have, lady : if it will please Cæsar
To be so good to Cæsar as to hear me,
I shall beseech him to befriend himself.

Por. Why, know'st thou any harm's intended towards
him?

Artem. None that I know will be, much that I fear may
chance.

Good morrow to you. — Here the street is narrow :
The throng that follows Cæsar at the heels,
Of Senators, of Prætors, common suitors,
Will crowd a feeble man almost to death :
I'll get me to a place more void, and there
Speak to great Cæsar as he comes along.   [*Exit*.

Por. I must go in. — [*Aside*.]   Ah me, how weak a thing
The heart of woman is ! — O Brutus,
The Heavens speed thee in thine enterprise ! —
Sure, the boy heard me. — Brutus hath a suit
That Cæsar will not grant.[5] — O, I grow faint. —
Run, Lucius, and commend me to my lord ;
Say I am merry : come to me again,
And bring me word what he doth say to thee.   [*Exeunt*.

---

[5] These words Portia speaks aloud to Lucius, as a blind to cover the true
cause of her uncontrollable flutter of spirits.

ACT III.

SCENE I. — *Rome.   Before the Capitol; the* Senate *sitting.*

A crowd of People in the street leading to the Capitol; among them ARTEMIDORUS, *and the* Soothsayer. *Flourish.   Enter* CÆSAR, BRUTUS, CASSIUS, CASCA, DECIUS, METELLUS, TRE-BONIUS, CINNA, ANTONY, LEPIDUS, POPILIUS, PUBLIUS, *and Others.*

Cæs. The Ides of March are come.

Sooth. Ay, Cæsar; but not gone.[1]

Artem. Hail, Cæsar! read this schedule.

Dec. Trebonius doth desire you to o'er-read,
At your best leisure, this his humble suit.

Artem. O Cæsar, read mine first; for mine's a suit
That touches Cæsar nearer: read it, great Cæsar.

Cæs. What touches us ourself shall be last served.

Artem. Delay not, Cæsar; read it instantly.[2]

---

[1] There was a certain soothsayer, that had given Cæsar warning long time afore, to take heed of the day of the Ides of March, which is the 15th of the month; for on that day he should be in great danger. That day being come, Cæsar, going into the Senate-house, and speaking merrily unto the soothsayer, told him " the Ides of March be come." — " So they be," softly answered the soothsayer, " but yet are they not past." — PLUTARCH.

[2] One Artemidorus also, born in the isle of Cnidos, a doctor of rhetoric in the Greek tongue, who by means of his profession was very familiar with certain of Brutus's confederates, and therefore knew the most part of all their practices against Cæsar, came and brought him a little bill, written with his own hand, of all that he meant to tell him. He, marking how Cæsar received all the supplications that were offered him, and that he gave them straight to his men that were about him, pressed nearer to him, and said: "Cæsar, read this memorial to yourself, and that quickly, for they be

Cæs. What, is the fellow mad?

Pub.   Sirrah, give place.

Cass. What, urge you your petitions in the street?
Come to the Capitol.[3]

CÆSAR *enters the Capitol, the rest following.   All the* Senators
rise.

Pop. I wish your enterprise to-day may thrive.

Cass. What enterprise, Popilius?

Pop. Fare you well.

Bru. What said Popilius Lena?

Cass. He wish'd to-day our enterprise might thrive.
I fear our purpose is discoverèd.

Bru. Look, how he makes to Cæsar : mark him.

Cass. Casca, be sudden, for we fear prevention. —
Brutus, what shall be done?   If this be known,
Cassius or Cæsar never shall turn back,
For I will slay myself.[4]

Bru.   Cassius, be constant :
Popilius Lena speaks not of our purpose ;
For, look, he smiles, and Cæsar doth not change.[5]

matters of great weight, and touch you nearly." Cæsar took it of him, but
could never read it, though he many times attempted it, for the number of
people that did salute him, but holding it still in his hand, keeping it to himself, went on withal to the Senate-house. — PLUTARCH.

[3] The murder of Cæsar did not, in fact, take place in the Capitol, as is
here represented, but in a hall or *Curia* adjoining Pompey's theatre, where
a statue of Pompey had been erected. The Senate had various places of
meeting; generally in the Capitol, occasionally in some one of the Temples,
at other times in one of the Curiæ, of which there were several in and about
the city.

[4] The meaning evidently is, "either Cassius or Cæsar shall never return
alive; for, if I do not kill him, I will slay myself."

[5] A senator called Popilius Lena after he had saluted Brutus and Cas-

Cass. Trebonius knows his time ; for, look you, Brutus,
He draws Mark Antony out of the way.

                    [*Exeunt* ANTONY *and* TREBONIUS. CÆSAR *and the*
                                        Senators *take their seats.*

Dec. Where is Metellus Cimber? Let him go,
And presently prefer his suit to Cæsar.

Bru. He is address'd :[6] press near and second him.

Cin. Casca, you are the first that rears your hand.

Casca. Are we all ready?

Cæs.   What is now amiss
That Cæsar and his Senate must redress?

Met. Most high, most mighty, and most puissant Cæsar,
Metellus Cimber throws before thy seat
An humble heart, —   [*Kneeling.*

---

sius more friendly than he was wont to do, he rounded softly in their ears,
and told them, "I pray the gods you may go through with that you have
taken in hand; but, withal, dispatch, I read you, for your enterprise is bewrayed." When he had said, he presently departed from them, and left
them both afraid that their conspiracy would out. — When Cæsar came out
of the litter, Popilius Lena went unto him, and kept him a long time with
talk. Cæsar gave good ear unto him; wherefore the conspirators, not hearing what he said, but conjecturing that his talk was none other but the very
discovery of their conspiracy, they were afraid every man of them; and one
looking in another's face, it was easy to see that they all were of a mind that
it was no tarrying for them till they were apprehended, but rather that they
should kill themselves with their own hands. And when Cassius and certain other clapped their hands on their swords under their gowns, to draw
them, Brutus marking the countenance and gesture of Lena, and considering that he did use himself rather like an humble and earnest suitor than
like an accuser, he said nothing to his companions, (because there were
many amongst them that were not of the conspiracy,) but with a pleasant
countenance encouraged Cassius; and immediately after, Lena went from
Cæsar, and kissed his hand, which showed plainly that it was for some
matter concerning himself that he had held him so long in talk. —
PLUTARCH.

    [6] *Address'd* is *ready, prepared.* Often so. See *Macbeth*, page 75, note 10.

Cæs.   I must prevent thee, Cimber.
These couchings [7] and these lowly courtesies
Might fire the blood of ordinary men,
And turn pre-ordinance and first decree
Into the play of children. [8]   Be not fond,
To think [9] that Cæsar bears such rebel blood
That will be thaw'd from the true quality
With that which melteth fools ; I mean, sweet words,
Low-crookèd curtsies, and base spaniel-fawning.
Thy brother by decree is banishèd :
If thou dost bend, and pray, and fawn for him,
I spurn thee like a cur out of my way.

Met.   Cæsar, thou dost me wrong.

Cæs.   Cæsar did never wrong but with just cause, [10]
Nor without cause will he be satisfied.

Met.   Is there no voice more worthy than my own,
To sound more sweetly in great Cæsar's ear
For the repealing [11] of my banish'd brother ?

[7] Among the proper senses of to *couch*, Richardson gives "to lower, to stoop, to bend down" ; and he says that "to *couch* and to *lower* have similar applications, and probably the same origin."

[8] "Pre-ordinance and first decree" is, I take it, the ruling or enactment of the highest authority in the State. "The play of children" here referred to is, as soon as they have done a thing, to turn round and undo it, or to build a house of blocks or cobs for the mere fun of knocking it over.

[9] "Be not *so* fond *as* to think," is the language in full. The Poet often omits the adverbs in such cases. *Fond,* here, is *foolish ;* which was its ordinary sense in Shakespeare's time.

[10] Metellus and Cæsar here use *wrong* in different senses. But to *hurt,* to *offend,* to *cause pain* were among its legitimate meanings in Shakespeare's time. So he has it afterwards in this play : "It shall advantage more than do us *wrong.*" And so in several other places ; as in *Othello,* ii. 3 : "I persuade myself, to speak the truth shall nothing *wrong* him." To *wring* and to *wrest* are from the same root as *wrong.* See Critical Notes.

[11] To *repeal* from banishment is, in old English, to *recall* by repealing the sentence. See *Richard the Second,* page 84, note 8.

Bru. I kiss thy hand, but not in flattery, Cæsar ;
Desiring thee that Publius Cimber may
Have an immediate freedom of repeal.

Cæs. What, Brutus !

Cass.   Pardon, Cæsar ; Cæsar, pardon :
As low as to thy foot doth Cassius fall,
To beg enfranchisement for Publius Cimber.

Cæs. I could be well moved, if I were as you ;
If I could pray to move, prayers would move me : [12]
But I am constant as the northern star,
Of whose true-fix'd and resting quality
There is no fellow in the firmament.
The skies are painted with unnumber'd sparks,
They are all fire, and every one doth shine ;
But there's but one in all doth hold his place :
So in the world ; 'tis furnish'd well with men,
And men are flesh and blood, and apprehensive ; [13]
Yet in the number I do know but one
That unassailable holds on his rank,
Unshaked of motion : [14] and that I am he,
Let me a little show it even in this, —
That I was constant Cimber should be banish'd,
And constant do remain to keep him so. [15]

[12] " If I could seek to move others by prayers, then I were capable of being myself moved by the prayers of others."

[13] *Apprehensive* is *intelligent, capable of apprehending.*

[14] " Unshaked of motion " is simply *unmoved*, or *not subject to motion.* Undisturbed *by* the motion of others. As all readers of the Bible know, *of* was continually used, with passive verbs, to denote the agent.

[15] All through this scene, Cæsar is made to speak quite out of character, and in a strain of hateful arrogance, in order, apparently, to soften the enormity of his murder, and to grind the daggers of the assassins to a sharper point. Perhaps, also, it is a part of the irony which so marks this play, to put the haughtiest words in Cæsar's mouth just before his fall. — It

Cin.   O Cæsar, —

Cæs.   Hence ! wilt thou lift up Olympus ?

Dec.   Great Cæsar, —

Cæs.   Doth not Brutus bootless kneel ?

Casca.   Speak, hands, for me !

[CASCA *stabs* CÆSAR *in the neck.* CÆSAR *catches hold*
     of his arm. He is then stabbed by several other
     Conspirators, *and at last by* MARCUS BRUTUS.

Cæs.   Et tu, Brute ? [16] — Then fall, Cæsar ! [17]

[*Dies. The* Senators *and* People *retire in confusion.*

may be well to add, that the carrying of deadly weapons was unlawful in
Rome; but every educated citizen carried a stylus in a sheath; and on this
occasion the assassins had daggers hidden in their stylus-cases.

[16] There is no classical authority for putting these words into the mouth
of Cæsar; and the English equivalent, *Thou too, Brutus,* sounds so much
better, that it seems a pity the Poet did not write so. Cæsar had been as a
father to Brutus, who was fifteen years his junior; and the Greek, *Kai su
teknon,* "You too, my son," which Dion and Suetonius put into his mouth,
though probably unauthentic, is good enough to be true.

[17] Trebonius drew Antonius aside, as he came into the house where the
Senate sat, and held him with a long talk without. When Cæsar was come
into the house, all the Senate rose to honour him at his coming in. So,
when he was set, the conspirators flocked about him, and amongst them
they presented one Metellus Cimber, who made humble suit for the calling
home again of his brother that was banished. They all made as though
they were intercessors for him, and took Cæsar by the hands, and kissed his
head and breast. Cæsar at first simply refused their kindness and entreaties;
but afterwards, perceiving they still pressed on him, he violently thrust them
from him. Then Cimber with both his hands plucked Cæsar's gown over
his shoulders, and Casca, that stood behind him, drew his dagger first and
struck Cæsar upon the shoulder, but gave him no great wound. Cæsar,
feeling himself hurt, took him straight by the hand he held his dagger in,
and cried out in Latin : "O traitor Casca, what doest thou ? " Casca on the
other side cried in Greek, and called his brother to help him. So divers
running on a heap together to fly upon Cæsar, he, looking about him to
have fled, saw Brutus with a sword drawn in his hand ready to strike at
him : then he let Casca's hand go, and, casting his gown over his face, suffered every man to strike at him that would. Then the conspirators throng-

Cin. Liberty! Freedom! Tyranny is dead! —
Run hence, proclaim, cry it about the streets.

Cass. Some to the common pulpits, and cry out,
Liberty, freedom, and enfranchisement! [18]

Bru. People, and Senators, be not affrighted;
Fly not; stand still { ambition's debt is paid.)

Casca. Go to the pulpit, Brutus.

Dec. And Cassius too.

Bru. Where's Publius?

Cin. Here, quite confounded with this mutiny.

Met. Stand fast together, lest some friend of Cæsar's
Should chance —

Bru. Talk not of standing. — Publius, good cheer!
There is no harm intended to your person,
Nor to no Roman else: so tell them, Publius.

Cass. And leave us, Publius; lest that the people,
Rushing on us, should do your age some mischief.

Bru. Do so; — and let no man abide [19] this deed,
But we the doers.

Re-enter TREBONIUS.

Cass. Where's Antony?

Tre. Fled to his house amazed.
Men, wives, and children stare, cry out, and run,
As it were doomsday.

---

ing one upon another, because every man was desirous to have a cut at
him, so many swords and daggers lighting upon one body, one of them
hurt another, and among them Brutus caught a blow on his hand, because
he would make one in murdering of him, and all the rest also were every
man of them bloodied. — PLUTARCH.

[18] This is somewhat in the style of Caliban, when he gets glorious with
"celestial liquor," *The Tempest*, ii. 2: "Freedom, hey-day! hey-day, freedom! freedom, hey-day, freedom!"

[19] To *abide* a thing is to stand responsible for it, to bear the consequences.

Bru.   Fates, we will know your pleasures :
That we shall die, we know ; 'tis but the time,
And drawing days out, that men stand upon.[20]

Casca. Why, he that cuts off twenty years of life
Cuts off so many years of fearing death.

Bru. Grant that, and then is death a benefit :
So are we Cæsar's friends, that have abridged
His time of fearing death. — Stoop, Romans, stoop,
And let us bathe our hands in Cæsar's blood
Up to the elbows, and besmear our swords :
Then walk we forth, even to the market-place,
And, waving our red weapons o'er our heads,
Let's all cry, *Peace, Freedom, and Liberty !*

Cass. Stoop, then, and wash.   How many ages hence
Shall this our lofty scene be acted o'er
In States unborn and accents yet unknown !

Bru. How many times shall Cæsar bleed in sport,
That now on Pompey's basis lies along[21]
No worthier than the dust !

Cass.   So oft as that shall be,
So often shall the knot of us be call'd
The men that gave their country liberty.[22]

Dec. What, shall we forth?

[20] "We all know that we are to die some time; and how long we can
draw out our life, is the only thing we concern ourselves about."

[21] So it was in fact: Cæsar fell at the pedestal of Pompey's statue; the
statue itself dripping with the blood that spurted from him.

[22] These three speeches, vain-gloriously anticipating the stage celebrity
of the deed, are very strange; and, unless there be a shrewd irony lurking
in them, I am at a loss to understand the purpose of them. Their effect on
my mind has long been to give a very ambitious air to the work of these
professional patriots, and to cast a highly theatrical colour on their alleged
virtue; as if they had sought to immortalize themselves by " striking the
foremost man of all this world,"

Cass.   Ay, every man away :
Brutus shall lead ; and we will grace his heels
With the most boldest[23] and best hearts of Rome.

Bru. Soft ! who comes here ?

Enter a Servant.

                                A friend of Antony's.

Serv. Thus, Brutus, did my master bid me kneel ;
Thus did Mark Antony bid me fall down ;
And, being prostrate, thus he bade me say :
Brutus is noble, wise, valiant, and honest ;
Cæsar was mighty, bold, royal, and loving :
Say I love Brutus, and I honour him ;
Say I fear'd Cæsar, honour'd him, and loved him.
If Brutus will vouchsafe that Antony
May safely come to him, and be resolved[24]
How Cæsar hath deserved to lie in death,
Mark Antony shall not love Cæsar dead
So well as Brutus living ; but will follow
The fortunes and affairs of noble Brutus
Thorough[25] the hazards of this untrod state
With all true faith.   So says my master Antony.

Bru. Thy master is a wise and valiant Roman ;
I never thought him worse.
Tell him, so please him come unto this place,
He shall be satisfied ; and, by my honour,
Depart untouch'd.

---

[23] This doubling of superlatives, as also of comparatives, and of nega-
tives, was very common in the Poet's time.   So, in The Acts, xxvi. 5, St. Paul
says, " after the *most strictest* sect of our religion I lived a Pharisee."

[24] *Informed, assured, satisfied* are among the old senses of *resolved.*

[25] Shakespeare uses *through* or *thorough* indifferently, as suits his verse
The two are in fact but different forms of the same word.

Serv.   I'll fetch him presently.   [*Exit.*

Bru. I know that we shall have him well to friend.

Cass. I wish we may : but yet have I a mind
That fears him much ; and my misgiving still
Falls shrewdly to the purpose.

Bru. But here comes Antony. —

Re-enter ANTONY.

Welcome, Mark Antony.

Ant. O mighty Cæsar ! dost thou lie so low?
Are all thy conquests, glories, triumphs, spoils,
Shrunk to this little measure?   Fare thee well. —
I know not, gentlemen, what you intend,
Who else must be let blood, who else is rank :[26]
If I myself, there is no hour so fit
As Cæsar's death-hour ; nor no instrument
Of half that worth as those your swords, made rich
With the most noble blood of all this world.
I do beseech ye, if you bear me hard,
Now, whilst your purpled hands do reek and smoke,
Fulfil your pleasure.   Live a thousand years,[27]
I shall not find myself so apt to die :
No place will please me so, no mean of death,
As here by Cæsar, and by you[28] cut off,
The choice and master spirits of this age.

[26] " Must be let blood " is a mere euphemism for " must be put to death."
— " Who else is rank " means " who else has too much blood in him." And
the idea is of one who has *overtopped* his equals, and *grown too high* for the
public safety. So in the speech of Oliver in *As You Like It*, i. 1, when incensed at the high bearing of Orlando : " Is it even so ? begin you to grow
upon me ?   I will physic your *rankness*."

[27] That is, " *if* I live," or " *should* I live, a thousand years."

[28] *By* is here used in two senses ; first, in the sense of *near*, or as a sign
of place ; second, to denote agency, as usual.

Bru. O Antony, beg not your death of us.
Though now we must appear bloody and cruel,
As, by our hands and this our present act,
You see we do ; yet see you but our hands,
And this the bleeding business they have done :
Our hearts you see not ; they are pitiful ;
And pity to the general wrong of Rome —
As fire drives out fire,[29] so pity pity —
Hath done this deed on Cæsar.   For your part,
To you our swords have leaden points, Mark Antony :
Our arms in strength of amity, and our hearts
Of brothers' temper, do receive you in
With all kind love, good thoughts, and reverence.

Cass. Your voice shall be as strong as any man's
In the disposing of new dignities.[30]

Bru. Only be patient till we have appeased
The multitude, beside themselves with fear,[31]

---

[29] As before noted, Shakespeare uses *fire* as one or two syllables indifferently, to suit his metre. Here the first *fire* is two syllables, the second one. — The allusion is to the old way of salving a burn by holding it up to the fire. So in *Romeo and Juliet*, i. 2 : "Tut, man, one fire burns out another's burning ; one pain is lessen'd by another's anguish."

[30] This little speech is snugly characteristic. Brutus has been talking about "our hearts," and "kind love, good thoughts, and reverence." To Cassius, all that is mere rose-water humbug, and he knows it is so to Antony too. He therefore hastens to put in such motives as he knows will have weight with Antony, as they also have with himself. And it is somewhat remarkable that several of these patriots, especially Cassius, the two Brutuses, and Trebonius, afterwards accepted the governorship of fat provinces for which they had been prospectively named by Cæsar ; they being of course too patriotic to resist the eloquence of such lucrative appointments.

[31] When Cæsar was slain, the Senate — though Brutus stood in the middest amongst them, as though he would have said something touching this fact — presently ran out of the house, and, flying, filled all the city with marvellous fear and tumult. — PLUTARCH.

And then we will deliver you the cause,
Why I, that did love Cæsar when I struck him,
Have thus proceeded.

\ *Ant.*   I doubt not of your wisdom.
Let each man render me his bloody hand :
First, Marcus Brutus, will I shake with you ; —
Next, Caius Cassius, do I take your hand ; —
Now, Decius Brutus, yours ; — now yours, Metellus ; —
Yours, Cinna ; — and, my valiant Casca, yours ; —
Though last, not least in love, yours, good Trebonius.
Gentlemen all, — alas, what shall I say ?
My credit now stands on such slippery ground,
That one of two bad ways you must conceit me,[32]
Either a coward or a flatterer. —
That I did love thee, Cæsar, O, 'tis true :
If, then, thy spirit look upon us now,
Shall it not grieve thee dearer[33] than thy death,
To see thy Antony making his peace,
Shaking the bloody fingers of thy foes, —
Most noble ! — in the presence of thy corse ?
Had I as many eyes as thou hast wounds,
Weeping as fast as they stream forth thy blood,
It would become me better than to close
In terms of friendship with thine enemies.
Pardon me, Julius ! Here wast thou bay'd,[34] brave hart ;
Here didst thou fall ; and here thy hunters stand,
Sign'd in thy spoil, and crimson'd in thy death. —

---

[32] Must *conceive of* me, or *construe me.* See page 71, note 40.

[33] Formerly *dear* might signify whatever moved any strong feeling, whether of pleasure or pain. The Poet has many instances of it used as here. See *Hamlet,* page 64, note 39.

[34] *Bay'd* is *brought to bay,* and so barked at and worried, as a deer by hounds. Shakespeare has the word often in that sense.

O world, thou wast the forest to this hart;
And this indeed, O world, the heart of thee. —
How like a deer, strucken by many princes,
Dost thou here lie !

    Cass. Mark Antony, —

    Ant.   Pardon me, Caius Cassius :
The enemies of Cæsar shall say this ;
Then, in a friend, it is cold modesty.[35]

    Cass. I blame you not for praising Cæsar so ;
But what compáct mean you to have with us?
Will you be prick'd [36] in number of our friends ;
Or shall we on, and not depend on you ?

    Ant. Therefore [37] I took your hands ; but was indeed
Sway'd from the point, by looking down on Cæsar.
Friends am I with you all, and love you all,
Upon this hope, that you shall give me reasons
Why and wherein Cæsar was dangerous.

    Bru. Or else were this a savage spectacle :
Our reasons are so full of good regard
That, were you, Antony, the son of Cæsar,
You should be satisfied.

    Ant.   That's all I seek :
And am moreover suitor that I may
Produce his body to the market-place ; [38]

---

[35] *Modesty* in its original sense of *moderation*. Frequent.

[36] *Prick'd* is *marked*. The image is of a list of names written out, and some of them distinguished by having holes pricked in the paper against them.

[37] *Therefore* is not the illative conjunction here; but means *to that end*, or *for that purpose*.

[38] *Produce* in the Latin sense of *produco ;* implying motion to a place. — Here, and all through this play, *market-place* is the *Forum*, where several rostra were provided for addressing the people. Shakespeare calls these rostra *pulpits.*

And in the pulpit, as becomes a friend,
Speak in the order of his funeral.

    Bru. You shall, Mark Antony.

    Cass.   Brutus, a word with you.

    [*Aside to* BRU.] You know not what you do; do not consent

That Antony speak in his funeral:
Know you how much the people may be moved
By that which he will utter?

    Bru. [*Aside to* CASS.]   By your pardon:
I will myself into the pulpit first,
And show the reason of our Cæsar's death:
What Antony shall speak, I will protest
He speaks by leave and by permission;
And that we are contented Cæsar shall
Have all due rights and lawful ceremonies.
It shall advantage more than do us wrong.[39]

    Cass. [*Aside to* BRU.] I know not what may fall; I like
      it not.

    Bru. Mark Antony, here, take you Cæsar's body.
You shall not in your funeral speech blame us,
But speak all good you can devise of Cæsar;
And say you do't by our permission;
Else shall you not have any hand at all
About his funeral: and you shall speak
In the same pulpit whereto I am going,
After my speech is ended.

---

[39] For this use of *wrong*, see page 104, note 10. — Note the high self-appreciation of Brutus here, in supposing that if he can but have a chance to speak to the people, and to air his wisdom before them, all will go right. Here, again, he overbears Cassius, who now begins to find the effects of having stuffed him with flatteries, and served as a mirror to "turn his hidden worthiness into his eye."

Ant.   Be it so ;
I do desire no more.

   Bru. Prepare the body, then, and follow us.

                  [*Exeunt all but* ANTONY.

   Ant. O, pardon me, thou bleeding piece of earth,
That I am meek and gentle with these butchers !
Thou art the ruins of the noblest man
That ever livèd in the tide of times.
Woe to the hands that shed this costly blood !
Over thy wounds now do I prophesy, —
Which, like dumb mouths, do ope their ruby lips,
To beg the voice and utterance of my tongue, —
A curse shall light upon the limbs of men ;[40]
Domestic fury and fierce civil strife
Shall cumber all the parts of Italy ;
Blood and destruction shall be so in use,
And dreadful objects so familiar,
That mothers shall but smile when they behold
Their infants quarter'd with the hands of war ;
All pity choked[41] with custom of fell deeds :
And Cæsar's spirit, ranging for revenge,
With Até[42] by his side come hot from Hell,
Shall in these confines with a monarch's voice
Cry *Havoc !* and let slip the dogs of war ;[43]

[40] By *men* Antony means not mankind in general ; the scope of the curse being limited by the subsequent words, " the parts of Italy," and " in these confines." — *Limbs* is merely the figure of speech called *Synecdoche,* or the putting of a part of a thing for the whole.

[41] " All pity *being* choked." Ablative absolute again.

[42] Até is the old goddess of discord and mischief. So, in *Much Ado,* ii. 1, Benedick describes Beatrice as " the infernal Até in good apparel."

[43] *Havoc* was anciently the word of signal for giving no quarter in a battle. It was a high crime for any one to give the signal without authority from the general-in-chief ; hence the peculiar force of *monarch's voice.* — To

That this foul deed shall smell above the earth
With carrion men, groaning for burial. —

Enter a Servant.

You serve Octavius Cæsar, do you not?

Serv. I do, Mark Antony.

Ant. Cæsar did write for him to come to Rome.

Serv. He did receive his letters, and is coming;
And bid me say to you by word of mouth, —
[*Seeing the body.*] O Cæsar ! —

Ant. Thy heart is big, get thee apart and weep.
Passion, I see, is catching; for mine eyes,
Seeing those beads of sorrow stand in thine,
Begin to water. Is thy master coming?

Serv. He lies to-night within seven leagues of Rome.

Ant. Post back with speed, and tell him what hath chanced.
Here is a mourning Rome, a dangerous Rome,
No Rome of safety [44] for Octavius yet;
Hie hence, and tell him so. Yet, stay awhile;
Thou shalt not back till I have borne this corse
Into the market-place : there shall I try,
In my oration, how the people take
The cruel issue of these bloody men;
According to the which, thou shalt discourse
To young Octavius of the state of things.
Lend me your hand. [*Exeunt with* CÆSAR'S *body.*

let slip a dog was a term of the chase, for releasing the hounds from the
leash or *slip* of leather whereby they were held in hand till it was time to let
them pursue the animal. — The *dogs of war* are fire, sword, and famine. So
in *King Henry V.*, first Chorus : "At his heels, *leash'd* in like *hounds*, should
famine, *sword*, and *fire*, crouch for employment."

[44] Another play on *Rome* and *room*. See page 53, note 38.

SCENE II. — *The Same.　The Forum.*

Enter BRUTUS *and* CASSIUS, *with a Throng of* Citizens.

Citizens. We will be satisfied ; let us be satisfied.

Bru. Then follow me, and give me audience, friends. —
Cassius, go you into the other street,
And part the numbers. —
Those that will hear me speak, let 'em stay here ;
Those that will follow Cassius, go with him ;
And public reason shall be renderéd
Of Cæsar's death.

1 Cit.　　　　　　I will hear Brutus speak.

2 Cit. I will hear Cassius ; and compare their reasons,
When severally we hear them renderéd.

　　　　[*Exit* CASSIUS, *with some of the* Citizens.　BRUTUS
　　　　　　　　　　　　goes into the Rostrum.

3 Cit. The noble Brutus is ascended : silence !

Bru. Be patient till the last.
Romans, countrymen, and lovers ![1] hear me for my cause ;
and be silent, that you may hear : believe me for mine honour ; and have respect to mine honour, that you may believe :
censure[2] me in your wisdom ; and awake your senses, that
you may the better judge. If there be any in this assembly,
any dear friend of Cæsar's, to him I say that Brutus' love to
Cæsar was no less than his. If, then, that friend demand
why Brutus rose against Cæsar, this is my answer, — Not
that I loved Cæsar less, but that I loved Rome more. Had

---

[1] *Lover* and *friend* were used as synonymous in the Poet's time. Brutus
afterwards speaks of Cæsar as " my best *lover.*"

[2] *Censure* is here, as often, *judge ;* probably used for the jingle it makes
with *senses.*

you rather Cæsar were living, and die all slaves, than that Cæsar were dead, to live all freemen? As Cæsar loved me, I weep for him; as he was fortunate, I rejoice at it; as he was valiant, I honour him: but, as he was ambitious, I slew him. There is tears for his love; joy for his fortune; honour for his valour; and death for his ambition. (Who is here so base that would be a bondman?) If any, speak; for him have I offended. Who is here so rude that would not be a Roman? If any, speak; for him have I offended. Who is here so vile that will not love his country? If any, speak; for him have I offended. I pause for a reply.

Citizens. None, Brutus, none.

Bru. Then none have I offended. I have done no more to Cæsar than you shall do to Brutus. The question of his death is enroll'd in the Capitol;[3] his glory not extenuated, wherein he was worthy; nor his offences enforced,[4] for which he suffered death.

Enter ANTONY and Others, with CÆSAR'S body.

Here comes his body, mourn'd by Mark Antony; who, though he had no hand in his death, shall receive the benefit of his dying, a place in the commonwealth; as which of you shall not? With this I depart, — That, as I slew my best lover for the good of Rome, I have the same dagger for myself, when it shall please my country to need my death.[5]

---

[3] The *reason* of his death is made a matter of solemn official record in the books of the Senate, as showing that the act of killing him was done for public ends, and not from private hate.

[4] His fame is not *lessened* or *whittled down in those points* wherein he was worthy. — *Enforced* is in antithesis to *extenuated*, meaning that his faults are not magnified or forced out of just measure.

[5] A great number of men being assembled together, Brutus made an

Citizens. Live, Brutus ! live, live !

1 Cit. Bring him with triumph home unto his house.

2 Cit. Give him a statue with his ancestors.

3 Cit. Let him be Cæsar.

4 Cit.   Cæsar's better parts
Shall now be crown'd in Brutus.

1 Cit. We'll bring him to his house with shouts and clam-
      ours.

Bru. My countrymen, —

2 Cit.   Peace ! silence ! Brutus speaks.

1 Cit. Peace, ho !

Bru. Good countrymen, let me depart alone,
And, for my sake, stay here with Antony :
Do grace to Cæsar's corpse, and grace his speech
Tending to Cæsar's glory ; which Mark Antony,
By our permission, is allow'd to make.
I do entreat you, not a man depart,
Save I alone, till Antony have spoke.   [*Exit*.

1 Cit. Stay, ho ! and let us hear Mark Antony.

oration unto them, to win the favour of the people, and to justify that they
had done. All those that were by said they had done well, and cried unto
them that they should boldly come down from the Capitol; whereupon
Brutus and his companions came boldly down into the market-place. The
rest followed in troop, but Brutus went foremost, very honourably compassed in round about with the noblest men of the city, which brought
him from the Capitol, through the market-place, to the pulpit for orations.
When the people saw him in the pulpit, although they were a multitude of
all sorts, and had a good will to make some stir; yet, being ashamed to do
it, for the reverence they bare unto Brutus, they kept silence to hear what
he would say. When Brutus began to speak, they gave him quiet audience :
howbeit, immediately after, they shewed him that they were not all contented
with the murder. For when another, called Cinna, would have spoken, and
began to accuse Cæsar, they fell into a great uproar among them, and marvellously reviled him; insomuch that the conspirators returned again into
the Capitol. — PLUTARCH.

3 Cit. Let him go up into the public chair;
We'll hear him. — Noble Antony, go up.

Ant. For Brutus' sake, I am beholding [6] to you. [*Goes up.*

4 Cit. What does he say of Brutus?

3 Cit.   He says, for Brutus' sake,
He finds himself beholding to us all.

4 Cit. 'Twere best he speak no harm of Brutus here.

1 Cit. This Cæsar was a tyrant.

3 Cit.   Nay, that's certain:
We're bless'd, that Rome is rid of him.

2 Cit. Peace! let us hear what Antony can say.

Ant. You gentle Romans, —

Citizens.   Peace, ho! let us hear him.

Ant. Friends, Romans, countrymen, lend me your ears;
I come to bury Cæsar, not to praise him.
The evil that men do lives after them;
The good is oft interrèd with their bones: [7]
So let it be with Cæsar.   The noble Brutus
Hath told you Cæsar was ambitious: [8]
If it were so, it was a grievous fault;
And grievously hath Cæsar answer'd it.
Here, under leave of Brutus and the rest, —
For Brutus is an honourable man;
So are they all, all honourable men, —

[6] Shakespeare always uses *beholding*, the active form, for *beholden*, the passive.   Here, as elsewhere, it means *obliged*, of course.

[7] We have the same thought in *Henry the Eighth*, iv. 2: "Men's evil manners live in brass; their virtues we write in water."

[8] In Shakespeare's time, the ending *-tious*, and various others like it, when occurring at the end of a verse, was often pronounced as two syllables.   The same was the case with *-tion, -sion*, and divers others.   Many instances of the latter have already occurred in this play; as in the preceding scene: "And say you do't by our *permission*."   Also in a former scene: "Out of the teeth of *emulation*."   The usage occurs continually in Spenser.

Come I to speak in Cæsar's funeral.
He was my friend, faithful and just to me :
But Brutus says he was ambitious ;
And Brutus is an honourable man.
He hath brought many captives home to Rome,
Whose ransoms did the general coffers [9] fill :
Did this in Cæsar seem ambitious?
When that the poor have cried, Cæsar hath wept :
Ambition should be made of sterner stuff :
Yet Brutus says he was ambitious ;
And Brutus is an honourable man.
You all did see that on the Lupercal [10]
I thrice presented him a kingly crown,
Which he did thrice refuse : was this ambition?
Yet Brutus says he was ambitious ;
And, sure, he is an honourable [11] man.
I speak not to disprove what Brutus spoke,
But here I am, to speak what I do know.
You all did love him once, — not without cause :

[9] Cæsar's campaigns in Gaul put vast sums of money into his hands, a large part of which he kept to his own use, as indeed he might have kept it all; but he did also, in fact, make over much of it to the *public treasury*. This was a very popular act of course, as it lightened the taxation of the city.

[10] That is, on *the day* when the feast of Lupercalia was held.

[11] Of course these repetitions of *honourable man* are intensely ironical; and for that very reason the irony should be studiously kept out of the voice in pronouncing them. I have heard speakers and readers utterly spoil the effect of the speech by specially emphasizing the irony; the proper force of which, in this case, depends on its being so disguised as to seem perfectly unconscious. For, from the extreme delicacy of his position, Antony is obliged to proceed with the utmost caution, until he gets, and sees he has got, the audience thoroughly in his power. The consummate adroitness which he uses to this end is the great charm of this incomparable oration.

What cause withholds you, then, to mourn [12] for him? —
O judgment, thou art fled to brutish beasts, [13]
And men have lost their reason ! — Bear with me ;
My heart is in the coffin there with Cæsar,
And I must pause till it come back to me.

    1 Cit. Methinks there is much reason in his sayings.

    2 Cit. If thou consider rightly of the matter,
Cæsar has had great wrong.

    3 Cit.   Has he not, masters?
I fear there will a worse come in his place.

    4 Cit. Mark'd ye his words? He would not take the
       crown ;
Therefore 'tis certain he was not ambitious.

    1 Cit. If it be found so, some will dear abide it. [14]

    2 Cit. Poor soul ! his eyes are red as fire with weeping.

    3 Cit. There's not a nobler man in Rome than Antony.

    4 Cit. Now mark him ; he begins again to speak.

    Ant. But yesterday the word of Cæsar might
Have stood against the world : now lies he there,
And none so poor to do him reverence. [15]
O masters, if I were disposed to stir
Your hearts and minds to mutiny and rage,
I should do Brutus wrong, and Cassius wrong,
Who, you all know, are honourable men :
I will not do them wrong ; I rather choose
To wrong the dead, to wrong myself, and you,

---

  [12] To *mourn* for *from mourning*   Another gerundial infinitive.

  [13] *Brutish* is by no means tautological here ; the antithetic sense of *human* brutes being most artfully implied.

  [14] Here, again, to *abide* a thing is to *suffer for* it, or, as we now say, to *pay for* it.   See page 107, note 19.

  [15] And there are none so humble but that he is beneath their reverence, or too low for their regard.

Than I will wrong such honourable men.
But here's a parchment with the seal of Cæsar, —
I found it in his closet, — 'tis his will :
Let but the commons hear this testament, —
Which, pardon me, I do not mean to read, —
And they would go and kiss dead Cæsar's wounds,
And dip their napkins[16] in his sacred blood ;
Yea, beg a hair of him for memory,
And, dying, mention it within their wills,
Bequeathing it as a rich legacy
Unto their issue.

   4 Cit. We'll hear the will : read it, Mark Antony.

   Citizens. The will, the will ! we will hear Cæsar's will.

   Ant. Have patience, gentle friends, I must not read it ;
It is not meet you know how Cæsar loved you.
You are not wood, you are not stones, but men ;
And, being men, hearing the will of Cæsar,
It will inflame you, it will make you mad.
'Tis good you know not that you are his heirs ;
For, if you should, O, what would come of it !

   4 Cit. Read the will ! we'll hear it, Antony ;
You shall read us the will, — Cæsar's will !

   Ant. Will you be patient ? will you stay awhile ?
I have o'ershot myself to tell you of it :
I fear I wrong the honourable men
Whose daggers have stabb'd Cæsar ;[17] I do fear it.

---

[16] *Napkin* and *handkerchief* were used indifferently.

[17] Antony now sees that he has the people wholly with him, so that he is perfectly safe in stabbing the stabbers with these terrible words. — " I have o'ershot myself to tell you of it " is, " I have gone too far, and hurt my own cause, *in telling* you of it." The infinitive used gerundively again. We have a like expression in *Henry the Eighth*, i. 1 : "We may outrun, by violent swiftness, that which we run at, and *lose by over-running.*" See, also, *Macbeth*, page 74, note 8.

4 Cit. They were traitors : honourable men !

Citizens. The will ! the testament !

2 Cit. They were villains, murderers.   The will ! read the will !

Ant. You will compel me, then, to read the will?
Then make a ring about the corpse of Cæsar,
And let me show you him that made the will.
Shall I descend? and will you give me leave?

Citizens. Come down.

2 Cit. Descend.   [*He comes down.*

3 Cit. You shall have leave.

4 Cit. A ring ! stand round.

1 Cit. Stand from the hearse, stand from the body.

2 Cit. Room for Antony ! — most noble Antony !

Ant. Nay, press not so upon me ; stand far'[18] off.

Citizens. Stand back ; room ! bear back.

Ant. If you have tears, prepare to shed them now.
You all do know this mantle : I remember
The first time ever Cæsar put it on ;
'Twas on a Summer's evening, in his tent,
That day he overcame the Nervii.[19]
Look, in this place ran Cassius' dagger through :

---

[18] The Poet has *far'* for *further* repeatedly.   So in *The Winter's Tale,* iv. 3 : " Not hold thee of our blood, no, not our kin, *far' than* Deucalion off."

[19] This is the artfullest and most telling stroke in Antony's speech.   The Romans prided themselves most of all upon their military virtue and renown : Cæsar was their greatest military hero ; and his victory over the Nervii was his most noted military exploit.   It occurred during his second campaign in Gaul, in the Summer of the year B.C. 57, and is narrated with surpassing vividness in the second book of his *Bellum Gallicum.*   Of course the matter about the " mantle " is purely fictitious : Cæsar had on the civic gown, not the military cloak, when killed : and it was, in fact, the mangled toga that Antony displayed on this occasion : but the fiction has the effect of making the allusion to the victory seem perfectly artless and incidental.

See what a rent the envious[20] Casca made :
Through this the well-belovèd Brutus stabb'd ;
And, as he pluck'd his cursèd steel away,
Mark how the blood of Cæsar follow'd it, —
As rushing out of doors, to be resolved[21]
If Brutus so unkindly knock'd, or no ;
For Brutus, as you know, was Cæsar's angel :[22]
Judge, O you gods, how dearly Cæsar loved him !
This was the most unkindest cut of all ;
For, when the noble Cæsar saw him stab,
Ingratitude, more strong than traitors' arms,
Quite vanquish'd him : then burst his mighty heart ;
And, in his mantle muffling up his face,
Even at the base of Pompey's statua,
Which all the while ran blood,[23] great Cæsar fell.
O, what a fall was there, my countrymen !
Then I, and you, and all of us fell down,
Whilst bloody treason flourish'd over us.
O, now you weep ; and, I perceive, you feel

20 *Envious*, again, in its old sense of *malicious* or *malignant*.

21 *Resolved*, again, for *informed* or *assured*. See page 109, note 24.

22 *Angel* here means, apparently, his counterpart, his good genius, or a kind of better and dearer self. See page 76, note 16.

23 They that had conspired his death compassed him in on every side with their swords drawn in their hands, that Cæsar turned him nowhere but he was stricken at by some, and still had naked swords in his face, and was hackled and mangled among them, as a wild beast taken of hunters. For it was agreed among them that every man should give him a wound, because all their parts should be in this murder. Men report also, that Cæsar did still defend himself against the rest, running every way with his body : but when he saw Brutus with his sword drawn in his hand, then he pulled his gown over his head, and made no more resistance, and was driven either casually or purposedly, by the counsel of the conspirators, against the base whereupon Pompey's image stood, which ran all of a gore-blood till he was slain. — PLUTARCH.

The dint [24] of pity : these are gracious drops.
Kind souls, what, weep you, when you but behold
Our Cæsar's vesture wounded?   Look you here,
Here is himself, marr'd, as you see, with [25] traitors.

   1 Cit. O piteous spectacle !

   2 Cit. O noble Cæsar !

   3 Cit. O woeful day !

   4 Cit. O traitors, villains !

   1 Cit. O most bloody sight !

   2 Cit. We will be revenged.

   Citizens. Revenge, — about, — seek, — burn, — fire, —
kill, — slay, — let not a traitor live !

   Ant. Stay, countrymen.

   1 Cit. Peace there ! hear the noble Antony.

   2 Cit. We'll hear him, we'll follow him, we'll die with him.

   Ant. Good friends, sweet friends, let me not stir you up
To such a sudden flood of mutiny.
They that have done this deed are honourable :
What private griefs [26] they have, alas, I know not,
That made them do't ; they're wise and honourable,
And will, no doubt, with reasons answer you.
I come not, friends, to steal away your hearts :
I am no orator, as Brutus is ;
But, as you know me all, a plain blunt man,
That love my friend ; and that they know full well
That gave me public leave to speak of him :
For I have neither wit, [27] nor words, nor worth,

---

   [24] *Dint* is, properly, *blow* or *stroke;* here put for the *impression* made by the blow.

   [25] *With*, again, as often, instead of *by*, to denote the relation of agent. *Marr'd* is *mangled*. See note 23.

   [26] *Griefs*, again, for *grievances*. See page 69, note 31.

   [27] *Wit* formerly meant *understanding*, and was so used by all writers.

Action, nor utterance, nor the power of speech,
To stir men's blood : I only speak right on ;
I tell you that which you yourselves do know ;
Show you sweet Cæsar's wounds, poor, poor dumb mouths,
And bid them speak for me : but were I Brutus,
And Brutus Antony, there were an Antony
Would ruffle up your spirits, and put a tongue
In every wound of Cæsar, that should move
The stones of Rome to rise and mutiny.

 Citizens. We'll mutiny.

 1 Cit. We'll burn the house of Brutus.

 3 Cit. Away, then ! come, seek the conspirators.

 Ant. Yet hear me, countrymen ; yet hear me speak.

 Citizens. Peace, ho ! hear Antony ; most noble Antony.

 Ant. Why, friends, you go to do you know not what.
Wherein hath Cæsar thus deserved your loves?
Alas, you know not ; I must tell you, then :
You have forgot the will I told you of.

 Citizens. Most true ; the will ! — let's stay, and hear the
   will.

 Ant. Here is the will, and under Cæsar's seal.
To every Roman citizen he gives,
To every several man, seventy-five drachmas.[28]

 2 Cit. Most noble Cæsar ! — we'll revenge his death.

 3 Cit. O, royal Cæsar !

 Ant. Hear me with patience.

 Citizens. Peace, ho !

 Ant. Moreover, he hath left you all his walks,

---

[28] The *drachma* was a Greek coin, equal to 7*d.* English. In fact, however, Cæsar left to each citizen three hundred sesterces, equivalent to about $14; which was practically as good as at least $100 in our time: no small lift for a poor man.

His private arbours, and new-planted orchards,
On this side Tiber :²⁹ he hath left them you,
And to your heirs for ever ; common pleasures,
To walk abroad, and recreate yourselves.
Here was a Cæsar ! when comes such another?

    1 Cit. Never, never. — Come, away, away !
We'll burn his body in the holy place,
And with the brands fire the traitors' houses.
Take up the body.

    2 Cit. Go, fetch fire.

    3 Cit. Pluck down benches.

    4 Cit. Pluck down forms,³⁰ windows, any thing.³¹

              [*Exeunt* Citizens, *with the body.*

---

²⁹ As this scene lies in the Forum, near the Capitol, Cæsar's gardens are, in fact, on *the other* side Tiber. But the Poet wrote as he read in Plutarch. See next note but one.

³⁰ A *form* is a *long seat*, like those in an audience-room or a school.

³¹ They came to talk of Cæsar's will and testament, and of his funerals and tomb. Then Antonius, thinking good his testament should be read openly, and also that his body should be honourably buried, and not in hugger-mugger, lest the people might thereby take occasion to be worse offended if they did otherwise ; Cassius stoutly spoke against it. But Brutus went with the motion, and agreed unto it ; wherein it seemeth he committed a second fault. For the first fault he did, was when he would not consent to his fellow-conspirators, that Antonius should be slain ; and therefore he was justly accused, that thereby he had saved and strengthened a strong and grievous enemy of their conspiracy. The second fault was, when he agreed that Cæsar's funerals should be as Antonius would have them, the which indeed marred all. For, first of all, when Cæsar's testament was openly read among them, whereby it appeared that he bequeathed unto every citizen of Rome 75 drachmas a man ; and that he left his gardens and arbours unto the people, which he had on this side of the river Tiber, in the place where now the temple of Fortune is built ; the people then loved him, and were marvellous sorry for him. Afterwards, when Cæsar's body was brought into the market-place, Antonius making his funeral oration in praise of the dead, according to the ancient custom of Rome, and perceiving that his words moved the common people to compassion, he framed his eloquence

Ant. Now let it work. — Mischief, thou art afoot,
Take thou what course thou wilt ! —

Enter a Servant.

How now, fellow !

Serv. Sir, Octavius is already come to Rome.

Ant. Where is he?

Serv. He and Lepidus are at Cæsar's house.

Ant. And thither will I straight to visit him :
He comes upon a wish. Fortune is merry,
And in this mood will give us any thing.

Serv. I heard 'em say, Brutus and Cassius
Are rid like madmen through the gates of Rome.

Ant. Belike they had some notice of the people,
How I had moved them. Bring me to Octavius. [*Exeunt.*

SCENE III. — *The Same. A Street.*

Enter CINNA, *the* Poet.

Cin. I dreamt to-night that I did feast with Cæsar,
And things unlucky charge my fantasy : [1]

to make their hearts yearn the more ; and taking Cæsar's gown all bloody in his hand, he laid it open to the sight of them all, shewing what a number of cuts and holes it had upon it. Therewithal the people fell presently into such a rage and mutiny, that there was no more order kept amongst the common people. For some of them cried out " Kill the murderers"; others plucked up forms, tables, and stalls about the market-place, as they had done before at the funerals of Clodius, and having laid them all on a heap together, they set them on fire, and thereupon did put the body of Cæsar, and burnt it in the midst of the most holy places. And furthermore, when the fire was throughly kindled, some here, some there, took burning fire-brands, and ran with them to the murderers' houses that killed him, to set them on fire. Howbeit the conspirators, foreseeing the danger before, had wisely provided for themselves and fled. — PLUTARCH.

[1] *Unlucky* is *ill-boding* or *portentous*. *Charge* is *burden* or *oppress*.

I have no will to wander forth of doors,
Yet something leads me forth.

Enter Citizens.

1 Cit. What is your name?

2 Cit. Whither are you going?

3 Cit. Where do you dwell?

4 Cit. Are you a married man or a bachelor?

2 Cit. Answer every man directly.

1 Cit. Ay, and briefly.

4 Cit. Ay, and wisely.

3 Cit. Ay, and truly; you were best.

Cin. What is my name? Whither am I going? Where do I dwell? Am I a married man or a bachelor? Then, to answer every man directly and briefly, wisely and truly. Wisely I say I am a bachelor.

2 Cit. That's as much as to say, they are fools that marry; you'll bear me a bang for that,[2] I fear. Proceed; directly.

Cin. Directly, I am going to Cæsar's funeral.

1 Cit. As a friend, or an enemy?

Cin. As a friend.

2 Cit. That matter is answered directly.

4 Cit. For your dwelling,—briefly.

Cin. Briefly, I dwell by the Capitol.

3 Cit. Your name, sir, truly.

Cin. Truly, my name is Cinna.

1 Cit. Tear him to pieces! he's a conspirator.

Cin. I am Cinna the poet, I am Cinna the poet.

4 Cit. Tear him for his bad verses, tear him for his bad verses.

Cin. I am not Cinna the conspirator.

---

[2] "You'll get a banging of me for that."

4 Cit. It is no matter; his name's Cinna: pluck but his name out of his heart, and turn him going.[3]

3 Cit. Tear him, tear him! Come; brands, ho! fire-brands! To Brutus', to Cassius'; burn all. Some to Decius' house, and some to Casca's; some to Ligarius': away, go! [*Exeunt.*

ACT IV.

SCENE I. — *Rome. A Room in* ANTONY'S *House.*[1]

ANTONY, OCTAVIUS, *and* LEPIDUS, *seated at a table.*

Ant. These many, then, shall die; their names are prick'd.

Oct. Your brother too must die: consent you, Lepidus?

[3] There was a poet called Cinna, who had been no partaker of the conspiracy, but was always one of Cæsar's chiefest friends: he dreamed, the night before, that Cæsar bad him to supper with him, and that, he refusing to go, Cæsar was very importunate with him, and compelled him; so that at length he led him by the hand into a great dark place, where, being marvellously afraid, he was driven to follow him in spite of his heart. This dream put him all night into a fever; and yet, notwithstanding, the next morning, when he heard that they carried Cæsar's body to burial, being ashamed not to accompany his funerals, he went out of his house, and thrust himself into the press of the common people that were in a great uproar. And because some one called him by his name Cinna, the people, thinking he had been that Cinna who in an oration he made had spoken very evil of Cæsar, they, falling upon him in their rage slew him outright in the market-place. — PLUTARCH.

[1] The time of this scene was, historically, in November, B.C. 43; some nineteen months after the preceding. — The place of the scene is shown to be at Rome, by Lepidus's being sent to Cæsar's house, and told that he will find his confederates "or here, or at the Capitol." In fact, however, the triumvirs, Octavius, Antonius, and Lepidus, did not meet at Rome to settle the proscription, but on a small island near Bologna. Plutarch relates the matter as follows: "All three met together in an island environed round

Lep. I do consent, —

Oct.   Prick him down, Antony.

Lep. — Upon condition Publius shall not live,
Who is your sister's son, Mark Antony.[2]

Ant. He shall not live; look, with a spot I damn[3] him.
But, Lepidus, go you to Cæsar's house;
Fetch the will hither, and we shall determine
How to cut off some charge in legacies.

Lep. What, shall I find you here?

Oct. Or here, or at the Capitol.   [*Exit* LEPIDUS.

Ant. This is a slight unmeritable[4] man,
Meet to be sent on errands : is it fit,
The threefold world divided, he should stand
One of the three to share it?

Oct.   So you thought him;
And took his voice who should be prick'd to die,

---

about with a little river, and there remained three days together. Now, as touching all other matters they were easily agreed, and did divide all the empire of Rome between them, as if it had been their own inheritance. But yet they could hardly agree whom they would put to death : for every one of them would kill their enemies, and save their kinsmen and friends. Yet, at length, giving place to their greedy desire to be revenged of their enemies, they spurned all reverence of blood and holiness of friendship at their feet. For Cæsar left Cicero to Antonius's will; Antonius also forsook Lucius Cæsar, who was his uncle by his mother; and both of them together suffered Lepidus to kill his own brother Paulus. Yet some writers affirm that Cæsar and Antonius requested Paulus might be slain, and that Lepidus was contented with it."

[2] According to Plutarch, as quoted in the preceding note, this was *Lucius* Cæsar, not *Publius;* nor was he Antony's *nephew,* but his uncle by the mother's side. A mistake by the Poet, probably.

[3] Both the verb to *damn* and the noun *damnation* were often used in the sense of to *condemn* simply. So it is, properly, in the English Bible.

[4] *Unmeritable* for *unmeriting* or *undeserving.* This indiscriminate use of active and passive forms, both in adjectives and participles, is very frequent in Shakespeare. The usage was common.

In our black sentence and proscription.

Ant. Octavius, I have seen more days than you:
And, though we lay these honours on this man,
To ease ourselves of divers slanderous loads,
He shall but bear them as the ass bears gold,
To groan and sweat under the business,
Either led or driven, as we point the way;
And having brought our treasure where we will,
Then take we down his load, and turn him off,
Like to the empty ass, to shake his ears,
And graze in commons.[5]

   Oct.   You may do your will;
But he's a tried and valiant soldier.

   Ant. So is my horse, Octavius; and for that
I do appoint him store of provender:
It is a creature that I teach to fight,
To wind,[6] to stop, to run directly on,
His corporal motion govern'd by my spirit.
And, in some taste, is Lepidus but so;
He must be taught, and train'd, and bid go forth:
A barren-spirited fellow; one that feeds
On objects, arts, and imitations,
Which, out of use and staled by other men,
Begin his fashion:[7] do not talk of him,

---

[5] *Commons*, here, is such pasture-lands as in England were not owned or appropriated by individuals, but occupied by a given neighbourhood *in common*.

[6] To *wind* is to *turn* or *bend* to the right or the left; the opposite of running "directly on," that is, *straight ahead*.

[7] That is, one who is always interested in, and talking about, such things — books, works of art, &c. — as everybody else has got tired of and thrown aside. So Falstaff's account of Shallow, in *2 Henry the Fourth*, iii. 2: "He came ever in the rearward of the fashion; and sung those tunes to the over-scutch'd huswives which he heard the carmen whistle, and sware they were

But as a property. And now, Octavius,
Listen great things : Brutus and Cassius
Are levying powers : we must straight make head : [8]
Therefore let our alliance be combined,
Our best friends made, our means stretch'd out ;
And let us presently go sit in council,
How covert matters may be best disclosed,
And open perils surest answeréd.

Oct. Let us do so : for we are at the stake,
And bay'd [9] about with many enemies ;
And some that smile have in their hearts, I fear,
Millions of mischiefs. 　　　　　　　　[*Exeunt.*

SCENE II. — *Before* BRUTUS' *Tent, in the Camp near Sardis.*[1]

Drum. Enter BRUTUS, LUCILIUS, TITINIUS, *and* SOLDIERS ;
　　PINDARUS *meeting them;* LUCIUS *at some distance.*

Bru. Stand, ho !
Lucil. Give the word, ho ! and stand.
Bru. What now, Lucilius ! is Cassius near?
Lucil. He is at hand ; and Pindarus is come
To do you salutation from his master.

　　　　　　[PINDARUS *gives a letter to* BRUTUS.

his Fancies or his Good-nights." In the text, *staled* is *outworn* or *grown
stale;* and the reference is not to objects, &c., generally, but only to those
which have lost the interest of freshness.

　[8] To *make head* is to *raise an army,* or to *lead one forth.* Often so.

　[9] An allusion to bear-baiting. One of the old English sports was, to tie
a bear to a stake, and then set a pack of dogs to barking at him and worry-
ing him. So in *Macbeth,* v. 7: "They've tied me to a stake; I cannot fly,
but, bear-like, I must fight the course." See, also, page 112, note 34.

　[1] This scene, again, is separated from the foregoing, historically, by about
a year; the remaining events of the drama having taken place in the Fall,
B.C. 42.

Bru. He greets me well. — Your master, Pindarus,
In his own charge, or by ill officers,[2]
Hath given me some worthy cause to wish
Things done, undone : but, if he be at hand,
I shall be satisfied.

Pin.   I do not doubt
But that my noble master will appear
Such as he is, full of regard and honour.

Bru. He is not doubted. — A word, Lucilius :
How he received you, let me be resolved.

Lucil. With courtesy and with respect enough ;
But not with such familiar instances,
Nor with such free and friendly conference,
As he hath used of old.

Bru.   Thou hast described
A hot friend cooling : ever note, Lucilius,
When love begins to sicken and decay,
It useth an enforcèd ceremony.
There are no tricks in plain and simple faith :
But hollow men, like horses hot at hand,[3]
Make gallant show and promise of their mettle ;
But, when they should endure the bloody spur,
They fall their crests, and, like deceitful jades,[4]
Sink in the trial.   Comes his army on ?

Lucil. They mean this night in Sardis to be quarter'd :
The greater part, the Horse in general,
Are come with Cassius.   [*March within.*

---

[2] That is, either by his own command, or by officers, subordinates, who
have abused their trust, prostituting it to the ends of private gain.

[3] Horses spirited or mettlesome when held back, or restrained.

[4] Here, as often, *fall* is transitive ; *let fall.* — A deceitful jade is an unre-
liable horse, or one that promises well in appearance, but " sinks in the
trial."

Bru.   Hark ! he is arrived.
March gently on to meet him.

Enter CASSIUS *and* Soldiers.

Cass.   Stand, ho !

Bru.   Stand, ho !   Speak the word along.

Within.   Stand !

Within.   Stand !

Within.   Stand !

Cass.   Most noble brother, you have done me wrong.

Bru.   Judge me, you gods ! wrong I mine enemies?
And, if not so, how should I wrong a brother?

Cass.   Brutus, this sober form of yours hides wrongs ;
And when you do them —

Bru.   Cassius, be content ;
Speak your griefs softly ; I do know you well.
Before the eyes of both our armies here,
Which should perceive nothing but love from us,
Let us not wrangle : bid them move away ;
Then in my tent, Cassius, enlarge [5] your griefs,
And I will give you audience.

Cass.   Pindarus,
Bid our commanders lead their charges [6] off
A little from this ground.

Bru.   Lucius, do you the like ; and let no man
Come to our tent, till we have done our conference. —
Lucilius and Titinius, guard our door.   [*Exeunt.*

---

[5] To *enlarge* is, properly, to *set free* or to *let go at large ;* here it means *speak freely of* or *unfold.*

[6] " Their *charges* " are, of course, the *troops* under their command.

SCENE III.—*Within the tent of* BRUTUS.

Enter BRUTUS *and* CASSIUS.

Cass. That you have wrong'd me doth appear in this:
You have condemn'd and noted [1] Lucius Pella
For taking bribes here of the Sardians;
Whereas my letters, praying on his side
Because I knew the man, were slighted off.

Bru. You wrong'd yourself to write [2] in such a case.

Cass. In such a time as this it is not meet
That every nice offence should bear his comment. [3]

Bru. And let me tell you, Cassius, you yourself
Are much condemn'd to have an itching palm;
To sell and mart your offices for gold
To undeservers.

Cass.   I an itching palm!
You know that you are Brutus that speak this,
Or, by the gods, this speech were else your last.

Bru. The name of Cassius honours this corruption,
And chastisement doth therefore hide his head.

Cass. Chastisement!

[1] That is, *disgraced* him, set a mark or stigma upon him.

[2] "Wrong'd yourself *by writing.*" The infinitive used gerundively again. So too in the second speech after, "condemn'd *to have*" is condemn'd *for having;* also "*to sell* and *mart,*" *for selling* and *marting.* The usage is uncommonly frequent in this play.

[3] *His* for *its,* as usual, referring to *offence.* The meaning is that every *petty* or *trifling* offence should not be rigidly scrutinized and censured. *Nice* was often used thus.—Cassius naturally thinks that "the honourable men whose daggers have stabb'd Cæsar" should not peril their cause by moral squeamishness. And it is a very noteworthy point, that the digesting of that act seems to have entailed upon Brutus a sort of moral dyspepsia. It appears, a little further on, that he is more willing to receive and apply money got by others than to use the necessary means of getting it.

Bru. Remember March, the Ides of March remember:
Did not great Julius bleed for justice' sake?
What villain touch'd his body, that did stab,
And not for justice?[4]   What! shall one of us,
That struck the foremost man of all this world
But for supporting robbers, — shall we now
Contaminate our fingers with base bribes,
And sell the mighty space of our large honours
For so much trash as may be graspèd thus?
I had rather be a dog, and bay the Moon,
Than such a Roman.[5]

  Cass.   Brutus, bay not me,
I'll not endure it: you forget yourself,
To hedge me in;[6] I am a soldier, ay,
Older in practice, abler than yourself

---

[4] Of course the meaning is, "Who of the stabbers was such a villain as to stab from any other motive than justice?"

[5] Brutus, upon complaint of the Sardians, did condemn and note Lucius Pella for a defamed person, that had been a Prætor of the Romans, and whom Brutus had given charge unto; for that he was accused and convicted of robbery and pilfery in his office. This judgment much misliked Cassius, because he himself had secretly (not many days before) warned two of his friends, attainted and convicted of the like offences, and openly had cleared them: but yet he did not therefore leave to employ them in any manner of service as he did before. And therefore he greatly reproved Brutus, for that he would shew himself so straight and severe, in such a time as was meeter to bear a little than to take things at the worst. Brutus in contrary manner answered, that he should remember the Ides of March, at which time they slew Julius Cæsar, who neither pilled nor polled the country, but only was a favourer and suborner of all them that did rob and spoil, by his countenance and authority. And if there were any occasion whereby they might honestly set aside justice and equity, they should have had more reason to have suffered Cæsar's friends to have robbed and done what wrong and injury they had would than to bear with their own men. — PLUTARCH.

[6] Still another gerundial infinitive: "*In hedging* me in."

To make conditions.[7]

 Bru.   Go to ;[8] you are not, Cassius.

 Cass. I am.

 Bru. I say you are not.

 Cass. Urge me no more, I shall forget myself;
Have mind upon your health, tempt me no further.

 Bru. Away, slight man!

 Cass. Is't possible?

 Bru.   Hear me, for I will speak.
Must I give way and room to your rash choler?
Shall I be frighted when a madman stares?

 Cass. O ye gods, ye gods! must I endure all this?

 Bru. All this! ay, more: fret, till your proud heart
   break;
Go show your slaves how choleric you are,
And make your bondmen tremble. Must I budge?
Must I observe you? Must I stand and crouch
Under your testy humour? By the gods,
You shall digest the venom of your spleen,[9]
Though it do split you; for from this day forth
I'll use you for my mirth, yea, for my laughter,
When you are waspish.

 Cass.   Is it come to this?

---

 [7] Now Cassius would have done Brutus much honour, as Brutus did unto him, but Brutus most commonly prevented him, and went first unto him, both because he was the elder man as also for that he was sickly of body. And men reputed him commonly to be very skilful in wars, but otherwise marvellous choleric and cruel, who sought to rule men by fear rather than with lenity.— PLUTARCH.

 [8] *Go to* is a phrase of varying import, sometimes of reproof, sometimes of encouragement. *Hush up, come on, go ahead, be off* are among its meanings. It was used a great deal, especially in colloquial speech.

 [9] The spleen was held to be the special seat of the sudden and explosive emotions and passions, whether of mirth or anger.

Bru. You say you are a better soldier :
Let it appear so ; make your vaunting true,
And it shall please me well : for mine own part,
I shall be glad to learn of abler men.

Cass. You wrong me every way, you wrong me, Brutus ;
I said an elder soldier, not a better : [10]
Did I say *better ?*

Bru.   If you did, I care not.

Cass. When Cæsar lived he durst not thus have moved
    me.

Bru. Peace, peace ! you durst not so have tempted him.

Cass. I durst not !

Bru. No.

Cass. What, durst not tempt him ?

Bru.   For your life you durst not.

Cass. Do not presume too much upon my love ;
I may do that I shall be sorry for.

Bru. You have done that you should be sorry for.
There is no terror, Cassius, in your threats ;
For I am arm'd so strong in honesty,
That they pass by me as the idle wind,
Which I respect not.   I did send to you
For certain sums of gold, which you denied me ; —
For I can raise no money by vile means :
By Heaven, I had rather coin my heart,

---

[10] This mistake of Brutus is well conceived. Cassius was much the abler
soldier, and Brutus knew it ; and the mistake grew from his consciousness
of the truth of what he thought he heard. Long before this time, Cassius
had served as Quæstor under Marcus Crassus in his expedition against
the Parthians ; and when the army was torn all to pieces, both Crassus and
his son being killed, Cassius displayed great ability in bringing off a rem-
nant ; as he also did for some time after that, in the military administration
of Syria.

And drop my blood for drachmas, than to wring
From the hard hands of peasants their vile trash
By any indirection [11] — I did send
To you for gold to pay my legions,
Which you denied me : was that done like Cassius?
Should I have answer'd Caius Cassius so?
When Marcus Brutus grows so covetous,
To lock such rascal counters [12] from his friends,
Be ready, gods, with all your thunderbolts,
Dash him to pieces !

   Cass.   I denied you not. [13]

   Bru. You did.

   Cass.   I did not : he was but a fool
That brought my answer back.   Brutus hath rived my heart :

---

[11] *Indirection* is, properly, *crookedness.* As the Latin *directus* is *straight*, hence *right*, so *indirectus* is *crooked*, hence *wrong.*

[12] "So covetous *as* to lock," of course. The Poet often omits *as* in such cases, for prosodical reasons. — *Rascal* was much used as a general term of contempt, meaning *worthless* or *base.* — *Counters* were round pieces of cheap metal used in making calculations. — Professor Dowden comments snugly on what we have here : " Brutus loves virtue and despises gold ; but in the logic of facts there is an irony cruel or pathetic. Brutus maintains a lofty position of immaculate honour above Cassius ; but ideals, and a heroic contempt for gold, will not fill the military coffer, or pay the legions ; and the poetry of noble sentiment suddenly drops down to the prosaic complaint that Cassius had denied the demands made by Brutus for certain sums of money. Nor is Brutus, though he worships an ideal of Justice, quite just in matters of concrete practical detail."

[13] Whilst Brutus and Cassius were together in the city of Smyrna, Brutus prayed Cassius to let him have part of the money whereof he had great store. Cassius's friends hindered this request, and earnestly dissuaded him from it ; persuading him, that it was no reason that Brutus should have the money which Cassius had gotten together by sparing, and levied with great evil will of the people their subjects, for him to bestow liberally upon his soldiers, and by this means to win their good wills, by Cassius's charge. Notwithstanding, Cassius gave him the third part of this total sum. — PLUTARCH.

A friend should bear his friend's infirmities,
But Brutus makes mine greater than they are.

Bru. I do not, till you practise them on me.

Cass. You love me not.

Bru.   I do not like your faults.

Cass. A friendly eye could never see such faults.

Bru. A flatterer's would not, though they did appear
As huge as high Olympus.

Cass. Come, Antony and young Octavius, come,
Revenge yourselves alone on Cassius,
For Cassius is a-weary of the world;
Hated by one he loves; braved[14] by his brother;
Check'd like a bondman; all his faults observed,
Set in a note-book, learn'd, and conn'd by rote,
To cast into my teeth.   O, I could weep
My spirit from mine eyes! — There is my dagger,
And here my naked breast; within, a heart
Dearer than Plutus' mine,[15] richer than gold:
If that thou be'st a Roman, take it forth;
I, that denied thee gold, will give my heart:
Strike as thou didst at Cæsar; for I know,
When thou didst hate him worst, thou lovedst him better
Than ever thou lovedst Cassius.

Bru.   Sheath your dagger:
Be angry when you will, it shall have scope;
Do what you will, dishonour shall be humour.[16]
O Cassius, you are yokèd with a lamb

---

14 *Braved* is *defied*, or treated with *bluster* and *bravado.*

15 Plutus is the old god of riches, who had all the world's gold in his keeping and disposal.

16 "Whatever dishonourable thing you may do, I will set it down to the humour or infirmity of the moment."

That carries anger as the flint bears fire ; [17]
Who, much enforcèd, shows a hasty spark,
And straight is cold again.

    Cass.   Hath Cassius lived
To be but mirth and laughter to his Brutus,
When grief, and blood ill-temper'd, vexeth him?

    Bru. When I spoke that, I was ill-temper'd too.

    Cass. Do you confess so much?   Give me your hand.

    Bru. And my heart too.

    Cass.   O Brutus, —

    Bru.   What's the matter?

    Cass. — Have you not love enough to bear with me,
When that rash humour which my mother gave me
Makes me forgetful?

    Bru.   Yes, Cassius ; and henceforth,
When you are over-earnest with your Brutus,
He'll think your mother chides, and leave you so.

                        [*Noise within.*

    Poet. [*Within.*] Let me go in to see the generals :
There is some grudge between 'em ; 'tis not meet
They be alone.

    Lucil. [*Within.*] You shall not come to them.

    Poet. [*Within.*] Nothing but death shall stay me.

    Enter Poet, *followed by* LUCILIUS *and* TITINIUS.

    Cass. How now !   What's the matter?

---

[17] In my boyhood, the idea was common, of fire *sleeping* in the flint, and being awaked by the stroke of the steel.   I am not sure whether it was known in the Poet's time, that in fact the flint cuts off microscopic bits of steel, which are ignited by the friction.   Hooker takes it as Shakespeare does; *Ecclesiastical Polity*, vii. 22, 3 : "It is not sufficient to carry religion in our hearts, as *fire is carried in flint-stones*, but we are outwardly, visibly apparently, to serve and honour the living God."

Poet. For shame, you generals ! what do you mean?
Love, and be friends, as two such men should be;
For I have seen more years, I'm sure, than ye.[18]

    Cass. Ha, ha ! how vilely doth this cynic rhyme !

    Bru. Get you hence, sirrah ; saucy fellow, hence !

    Cass. Bear with him, Brutus ; 'tis his fashion.

    Bru. I'll know his humour, when he knows his time :
What should the wars do with these jigging fools? —
Companion, hence ![19]

    Cass.   Away, away, be gone !   [*Exit* Poet.

[18] Before they fell in hand with any other matter, they went into a little chamber together, and bade every man avoid, and did shut the doors to them. Then they began to pour out their complaints one to the other, and grew hot and loud, earnestly accusing one another, and at length both fell a-weeping. Their friends that were without the chamber, hearing them loud within, and angry between themselves, were both amazed and afraid also, lest it would grow to further matter; but yet they were commanded that no man should come to them. Notwithstanding, one Marcus Favonius, that took upon him to counterfeit a philosopher, not with wisdom and discretion, but with a certain bedlam and frantic motion; he would needs come into the chamber, though the men offered to keep him out. But it was no boot to let Favonius, when a mad mood or toy took him in the head: for he was an hot hasty man, and sudden in all his doings, and cared for never a Senator of them all. Now, though he used this bold manner of speech after the profession of the Cynic philosophers, (as who would say, *Dogs*,) yet his boldness did not hurt many times, because they did but laugh at him to see him so mad. This Favonius at that time, in despite of the door-keepers, came into the chamber, and with a certain scoffing and mocking gesture, which he counterfeited of purpose, he re-hearsed the verses which old Nestor said in Homer: —

> My lords, I pray you hearken both to me,
> For I have seen mo years than suchie three.

Cassius fell a-laughing at him; but Brutus thrust him out of the chamber, and called him dog, and counterfeit Cynic. Howbeit his coming in brake their strife at that time, and so they left each other. — PLUTARCH.

[19] *Jig* signified a ballad or ditty, as well as a dance. *Companion* is here a term of contempt, as we now use *fellow*.

Bru. Lucilius and Titinius, bid the commanders
Prepare to lodge their companies to-night.

Cass. And come yourselves, and bring Messala with you
Immediately to us.   [*Exeunt* LUCILIUS *and* TITINIUS.

Bru.   Lucius, a bowl of wine !

Cass. I did not think you could have been so angry.

Bru. O Cassius, I am sick of many griefs.

Cass. Of your philosophy you make no use,
If you give place to accidental evils.[20]

Bru. No man bears sorrow better. Portia is dead.

Cass. Ha ! Portia !

Bru. She is dead.

Cass. How 'scaped I killing, when I cross'd you so ? —
O insupportable and touching loss ! —
Upon what sickness ?

Bru.   Impatient[21] of my absence,
And grief that young Octavius with Mark Antony
Have made themselves so strong ; — for with her death
That tidings came ; — with this she fell distract,[22]
And, her attendants absent, swallow'd fire.[23]

[20] In his philosophy, Brutus was a mixture of the Stoic and the Platonist.
What he says of Portia's death is among the best things in the play, and is
in Shakespeare's noblest style. Deep grief loves not many words.

[21] Strict harmony of construction would require *impatience* here, or else
grieved for *grief* in the next line. But the Poet is not very particular in
such matters. The sense is clear enough.

[22] *Distract* for *distracted*. The shortening of preterites in this way was
very common; and Shakespeare has many instances of it. See *Hamlet*,
page 165, note 32.

[23] It appears something uncertain whether Portia's death was before or
after her husband's. Plutarch represents it as occurring before; but Merivale follows those who place it after. Plutarch's account is as follows : " For
Portia, Brutus's wife, Nicolaus the philosopher and Valerius Maximus do
write, that she determining to kill herself (her friends carefully looking to
her to keep her from it) took hot burning coals, and cast them into her

Cass. And died so?

Bru. Even so.

Cass. O ye immortal gods!

Enter LUCIUS, *with wine and a taper.*

Bru. Speak no more of her. — Give me a bowl of wine. —
In this I bury all unkindness, Cassius.   [*Drinks.*

Cass. My heart is thirsty for that noble pledge. —
Fill, Lucius, till the wine o'erswell the cup;
I cannot drink too much of Brutus' love.   [*Drinks.*

Bru. Come in, Titinius! —   [*Exit* LUCIUS.

Re-enter TITINIUS, *with* MESSALA.

Welcome, good Messala. —
Now sit we close about this taper here,
And call in question[24] our necessities.

Cass. Portia, art thou gone?

Bru.   No more, I pray you. —
Messala, I have here receivèd letters,
That young Octavius and Mark Antony
Come down upon us with a mighty power,
Bending their expedition[25] toward Philippi.

Mes. Myself have letters of the selfsame tenour.

Bru. With what addition?

Mes. That, by proscription and bills of outlawry,
Octavius, Antony, and Lepidus,

---

mouth, and kept her mouth so close that she choked herself. There was a letter of Brutus found, written to his friends, complaining of their negligence, that, his wife being sick, they would not help her, but suffered her to kill herself, choosing to die rather than to languish in pain."

24 "Call in *question*" here means *talk* or *converse about*. *Question*, both as noun and verb, was often used in that sense.

25 *Directing* their *march*. So the Poet has *expedition* repeatedly.

Have put to death an hundred Senators.

Bru. Therein our letters do not well agree :
Mine speak of seventy Senators that died
By their proscriptions, Cicero being one.[26]

Cass. Cicero one !

Mes. Cicero is dead,
And by that order of proscription. —
Had you your letters from your wife, my lord?

Bru. No, Messala.

Mes. Nor nothing in your letters writ of her?

Bru. Nothing, Messala.[27]

Mes.   That, methinks, is strange.

Bru. Why ask you? hear you ought of her in yours?

Mes. No, my lord.

Bru. Now, as you are a Roman, tell me true.

Mes. Then like a Roman bear the truth I tell :
For certain she is dead, and by strange manner.

Bru. Why, farewell, Portia. — We must die, Messala :
With meditating that she must die once,[28]
I have the patience to endure it now.

Mes. Even so great men great losses should endure.

[26] These three, Octavius Cæsar, Antonius, and Lepidus, made an agreement among themselves, and by those articles divided the provinces belonging to the empire of Rome among themselves, and did set up bills of proscription and outlawry, condemning two hundred of the noblest men of
Rome to suffer death, and among that number Cicero was one.— PLU-
TARCH.

[27] This may seem inconsistent with what has gone before : but we are to
suppose that Brutus's friends at Rome did not write to him directly of Portia's death, lest the news might upset him too much ; but wrote to some
common friends in the army, directing them to break the news to him, as
they should deem it safe and prudent to do so.

[28] *Once* for *one time or other, sometime.* So in *The Merry Wives,* iii. 4 :
" I pray thee, *once* to-night give my sweet Nan this ring."

Cass. I have as much of this in art[29] as you,
But yet my nature could not bear it so.

Bru. Well, to our work alive.[30]   What do you think
Of marching to Philippi presently?

Cass. I do not think it good.

Bru.   Your reason?

Cass.   This it is:
'Tis better that the enemy seek us:
So shall he waste his means, weary his soldiers,
Doing himself offence; whilst we, lying still,
Are full of rest, defence, and nimbleness.

Bru. Good reasons must, of force,[31] give place to better.
The people 'twixt Philippi and this ground
Do stand but in a forced affection;
For they have grudged us contribution:
The enemy, marching along by them,
By them shall make a fuller number up,
Come on refresh'd, new-aided, and encouraged;
From which advantage shall we cut him off,
If at Philippi we do face him there,
These people at our back.

Cass.   Hear me, good brother.

---

[29] *Art* was sometimes used for *theory* as opposed to *practice*.

[30] Probably meaning "the work we have to do *with the living*."

[31] *Of force* is of *necessity*, or *necessarily*. — Plutarch represents this talk as occurring at Philippi just before the battle: "Cassius was of opinion not to try this war at one battle, but rather to delay time, and to draw it out in length, considering that they were the stronger in money, and the weaker in men and armour. But Brutus, in contrary manner, did always before and at that time also, desire nothing more than to put all to the hazard of battle, as soon as might be possible; to the end he might either quickly restore his country to her former liberty, or rid him forthwith of this miserable world, being still troubled in following and maintaining of such great armies together."

Bru. Under your pardon. You must note besides,
That we have tried the utmost of our friends,
Our legions are brim-full, our cause is ripe :
The enemy increaseth every day ;
We, at the height, are ready to decline.
There is a tide in the affairs of men,
Which, taken at the flood, leads on to fortune ;
Omitted, all the voyage of their life
Is bound in shallows and in miseries.
On such a full sea are we now afloat ;
And we must take the current when it serves,
Or lose our ventures.[32]

Cass.　　　　　Then, with your will, go on :
We will along ourselves, and meet them at Philippi.

Bru. The deep of night is crept upon our talk,
And nature must obey necessity ;
Which we will niggard with a little rest.
There is no more to say?

Cass.　　　　　No more.　Good night :
Early to-morrow will we rise, and hence.

Bru. Lucius, my gown !—Farewell now, good Messala :—
Good night, Titinius : — noble, noble Cassius,
Good night, and good repose.

Cass.　　　　　O my dear brother !
This was an ill beginning of the night :
Never come such division 'tween our souls !
Let it not, Brutus.

Bru.　　　　Every thing is well.

Cass. Good night, my lord.

---

[32] *Ventures* for what is *risked* or *adventured*. The figure of a ship is kept
up ; and *venture* denotes whatever is put on board, in hope of profit. The
Poet has it repeatedly so.

Bru.   Good night, good brother.

Tit.
Mes. } Good night, **Lord** Brutus.

Bru.   Farewell, every one. —

             [*Exeunt* CASSIUS, TITINIUS, *and* MESSALA.

        Re-enter LUCIUS, *with the gown.*

Give me the gown.   Where is thy instrument?

   Luc. Here in the tent.

   Bru.   What, thou speak'st drowsily :

Poor knave,[33] I blame thee not ; thou art o'er-watch'd.

Call Claudius and some other of my men ;

I'll have them sleep on cushions in my tent.

   Luc. Varro and Claudius !

        Enter VARRO *and* CLAUDIUS.

   Var. Calls my lord?

   Bru. I pray you, sirs, lie in my tent, and sleep ;

It may be I shall raise you by-and-by

On business to my brother Cassius.

   Var. So please you, we will stand and watch your pleasure.

   Bru. I will not have it so ; lie down, good sirs :

It may be I shall otherwise bethink me. —

Look, Lucius, here's the book I sought for so ;

I put it in the pocket of my gown.[34]   [*Servants lie down.*

   Luc. I was sure your lordship did not give it me.

   Bru. Bear with me, good boy ; I am much forgetful.

  [33] *Knave* was much used as a term of endearment, or of loving familiarity with those of lower rank.

  [34] These two simple lines are among the best things in the play. Just consider how much is implied in them, and what a picture they give of the earnest, thoughtful, book-loving Brutus. And indeed all his noblest traits of character come out, "in simple and pure soul," in this exquisite scene with Lucius, which is hardly surpassed by any thing in Shakespeare.

Canst thou hold up thy heavy eyes awhile,
And touch thy instrument a strain or two?

Luc. Ay, my lord, an't please you.

Bru. It does, my boy:
I trouble thee too much, but thou art willing.

Luc. It is my duty, sir.

Bru. I should not urge thy duty past thy might;
I know young bloods[35] look for a time of rest.

Luc. I have slept, my lord, already.

Bru. It was well done; and thou shalt sleep again;
I will not hold thee long: if I do live,
I will be good to thee. —

[LUCIUS *plays and sings till he falls asleep.*

This is a sleepy tune. — O murderous Slumber,
Lay'st thou thy leaden mace upon my boy,
That plays thee music?[36] — Gentle knave, good night;
I will not do thee so much wrong to wake thee:
If thou dost nod, thou breakst thy instrument;
I'll take it from thee; and, good boy, good night. —
Let me see, let me see; is not the leaf turn'd down
Where I left reading? Here it is, I think.

Enter the Ghost of CÆSAR.

How ill this taper burns![37] — Ha! who comes here?

[35] *Bloods* for *persons.* So in *Much Ado,* iii. 3: "How giddily he turns about all the hot *bloods* between fourteen and five-and-thirty."

[36] *Mace* was formerly used for *sceptre.* The mace is called *leaden,* from its causing heaviness in the subject of it. — Slumber has the epithet *murderous,* because sleep is regarded as the image of death; or, as Shelley puts it, "Death and his brother Sleep." — The boy is spoken of as playing music to Slumber, because the purpose of his music is to soothe the perturbations out of his master's mind, and put him to sleep.

[37] The coming of a ghost was believed to make lights burn dimly. So, in *Richard the Third,* v. 3, when the ghosts appear to Richard, he says, "The lights *burn blue.*"

I think it is the weakness of mine eyes
That shapes this monstrous apparition.
It comes upon me. — Art thou any thing?
Art thou some god, some angel, or some devil,
That makest my blood cold, and my hair to stare?[38]
Speak to me what thou art.

Ghost. Thy evil spirit, Brutus.

Bru.   Why comest thou?

Ghost. To tell thee thou shalt see me at Philippi.

Bru. Well; then I shall see thee again?

Ghost. Ay, at Philippi.

Bru. Why, I will see thee at Philippi, then.

                                   [*Ghost vanishes.*

Now I have taken heart, thou vanishest:[39]
Ill spirit, I would hold more talk with thee.[40] —

[38] A singular use of *stare*. Of course it must mean to *stick out*, or, as it is in *Hamlet*, to "*stand on end*, like quills upon the fretful porpentine." We have a similar expression in *The Tempest*, i. 2: "Ferdinand, with hair *up-staring*, — then like reeds, not hair."

[39] This strongly, though quietly, marks the Ghost as *subjective*: as soon as Brutus recovers his firmness, the illusion is broken. The order of things is highly judicious here, in bringing the "horrible vision" upon Brutus just after he has heard of Portia's shocking death. With that great sorrow weighing upon him, he might well see ghosts. The thickening of calamities upon him, as the consequences of his stabbing exploit, naturally awakens remorse.

[40] Above all, the ghost that appeared unto Brutus shewed plainly that the gods were offended with the murder of Cæsar. The vision was thus: Brutus, being ready to pass over his army from the city of Abydos to the other coast lying directly against it, slept every night (as his manner was) in his tent; and being yet awake, thinking of his affairs (for by report he was as careful a captain, and lived with as little sleep as ever man did) he thought he heard a noise at his tent-door, and, looking towards the light of the lamp that waxed very dim, he saw a horrible vision of a man, of a wonderful greatness and dreadful look, which at the first made him marvellously afraid. But when he saw that it did him no hurt, but stood at his bed-side and said

Boy! Lucius!—Varro! Claudius! Sirs, awake!—
Claudius!

Luc. The strings, my lord, are false.

Bru. He thinks he still is at his instrument. —
Lucius, awake!

Luc. My lord?

Bru. Didst thou dream, Lucius, that thou so criedst out?

Luc. My lord, I do not know that I did cry.

Bru. Yes, that thou didst: didst thou see any thing?

Luc. Nothing, my lord.

Bru. Sleep again, Lucius. — Sirrah Claudius! —
[*To* Var.]   Fellow thou, awake!

Var. My lord?

Clau. My lord?

Bru. Why did you so cry out, sirs, in your sleep?

Var. ⎫
Clau. ⎭ Did we, my lord?

Bru.   Ay: saw you any thing?

Var. No, my lord, I saw nothing.

Clau.   Nor I, my lord.

Bru. Go and commend me to my brother Cassius;
Bid him set on his powers betimes [41] before,
And we will follow.

Var. ⎫
Clau. ⎭ It shall be done, my lord.   [*Exeunt.*

---

nothing; at length he asked him what he was. The image answered him:
"I am thy ill angel, Brutus, and thou shalt see me by the city of Philippes."
Then Brutus replied again, and said, "Well, I shall see thee then." There-
withal the spirit presently vanished from him. — PLUTARCH.

[41] *Betimes* is *early, promptly*, or *in good time.*

(handwritten: 20 Here Shure)

ACT V.

SCENE I. — *The Plains of Philippi.*

Enter OCTAVIUS, ANTONY, *and their* Army.

Oct. Now, Antony, our hopes are answeréd.
You said the enemy would not come down,
But keep the hills and upper regions:
It proves not so; their battles [1] are at hand:
They mean to warn [2] us at Philippi here,
Answering before we do demand of them.

   Ant. Tut, I am in their bosoms, and I know
Wherefore they do it: they could [3] be content
To visit other places; and come down
With fearful bravery, [4] thinking by this face
To fasten in our thoughts that they have courage;
But 'tis not so.

Enter a Messenger.

   Mess.   Prepare you, generals:

---

[1] *Battle* was used for an *army*, especially an army *embattled*, or ordered in battle-array. The plural is here used with historical correctness, as Brutus and Cassius had each an army: the two armies of course co-operating, and acting together as one.

[2] To *warn* for to *summon*. So in *King John:* "Who is it that hath *warn'd* us to the walls?" And in *King Richard III.:* "And sent to *warn* them to his royal presence."

[3] *Could* for *would*. The auxiliaries *could*, *should*, and *would* were often used indiscriminately. — *Content*, here, means more than in our use, and has the sense of *be glad*, or *prefer*.

[4] *Bravery* is *bravado* or *defiance*. Often so. The epithet *fearful* probably means that fear is what thus puts them upon attempting to intimidate by display and brag.

The enemy comes on in gallant show;
Their bloody sign of battle is hung out,
And something to be done immediately.

Ant. Octavius, lead your battle softly on,
Upon the left hand of the even field.

Oct. Upon the right hand I; keep thou the left.

Ant. Why do you cross me in this exigent?

Oct. I do not cross you; but I will do so.[5] [*March.*

Drum. *Enter* BRUTUS, CASSIUS, *and their* Army; LUCILIUS,
TITINIUS, MESSALA, *and Others.*

Bru. They stand, and would have parley.

Cass. Stand fast, Titinius: we must out and talk.

Oct. Mark Antony, shall we give sign of battle?

Ant. No, Cæsar, we will answer on their charge.[6]
Make forth; the generals would have some words.

Oct. Stir not until the signal.

Bru. Words before blows: is it so, countrymen?

Oct. Not that we love words better, as you do.

Bru. Good words are better than bad strokes, Octavius.

---

[5] That is, "I will do as I have said"; not, "I will cross you."—At this
time, Octavius was but twenty-one years old, and Antony was old enough to
be his father. At the time of Cæsar's death, when Octavius was in his nine-
teenth year, Antony thought he was going to manage him easily and have
it all his own way with him, but he found the youngster as stiff as a crow-
bar, and could do nothing with him. Cæsar's youngest sister Julia was
married to Marcus Atius Balbus, and their daughter Atia, again, was married to Caius Octavius, a nobleman of the Plebeian order. From this marriage sprang the present Octavius, who afterwards became the Emperor
Augustus. He was mainly educated by his great-uncle, was advanced to
the Patrician order, and was adopted as his son and heir; so that his full
and proper designation at this time was Caius Julius Cæsar Octavianus.
The text gives a right taste of the man, who always stood firm as a post
against Antony, till the latter finally knocked himself to pieces against him.

[6] *Charge* for *attack*; and *answer* in the sense of *meet in combat.*

Ant. In your bad strokes, Brutus, you give good words :
Witness the hole you made in Cæsar's heart,
Crying, *Long live ! hail, Cæsar !*

   Cass.   Antony,
The posture of your blows are yet unknown ;[7]
But, for your words, they rob the Hybla bees,
And leave them honeyless.[8]

   Ant.   Not stingless too.

   Bru. O, yes, and soundless too ;
For you have stol'n their buzzing, Antony,
And very wisely threat before you sting.

   Ant. Villains, you did not so when your vile daggers
Hack'd one another in the sides of Cæsar :
You show'd your teeth like apes, and fawn'd like hounds,
And bow'd like bondmen, kissing Cæsar's feet ;
Whilst damnèd Casca, like a cur, behind
Struck Cæsar on the neck.   O flatterers !

   Cass. Flatterers ! — Now, Brutus, thank yourself :
This tongue had not offended so to-day,
If Cassius might have ruled.

   Oct. Come, come, the cause : if arguing makes us sweat,
The proof of it will turn to redder drops.
Look, —
I draw a sword against conspirators :
When think you that the sword goes up again?
Never, till Cæsar's three-and-thirty wounds

   [7] *Posture* for *nature* or *character*, probably; rather an odd use of the
word. — The verb *are* is made to agree with the nearest substantive, *blows*,
instead of with its proper nominative, *posture*. Such loosenesses of grammar
were common.   See *Hamlet*, page 57, note 12.

   [8] *Hybla* was the name of a place in Sicily, noted for the fine flavour of its
honey. — The meaning is, that Antony could not be so "honey-tongued,"
unless he had quite exhausted thyme-flavoured Hybla.

Be well avenged ;[9] or till another Cæsar
Have added slaughter to the sword of traitors.[10]

Bru. Cæsar, thou canst not die by traitor's hands,
Unless thou bring'st them with thee.

Oct.   So I hope ;
I was not born to die on Brutus' sword.

Bru. O, if thou wert the noblest of thy strain,[11]
Young man, thou couldst not die more honourably.

Cass. A peevish schoolboy, worthless of such honour,
Join'd with a masker and a reveller ![12]

Ant. Old Cassius still !

Oct.   Come, Antony ; away ! —
Defiance, traitors, hurl we in your teeth :
If you dare fight to-day, come to the field ;
If not, when you have stomachs.[13]

> [*Exeunt* OCTAVIUS, ANTONY, *and their* Army.

Cass. Why, now, blow wind, swell billow, and swim bark !

---

[9] The historical number of Cæsar's wounds is three-and-*twenty*, and so
Shakespeare read it in *Plutarch.* But the poets care little for exactness in
such matters. In Beaumont and Fletcher's *Two Noble Gentlemen*, we have
"Cæsar's *two-and-thirty* wounds." — This man, Octavius, has been a standing puzzle and enigma to the historians, from the seeming contradictions of
his character. The later writers, however, especially Merivale and Smith,
find that the one principle that gave unity to his life and reconciled those
contradictions, was a steadfast, inflexible purpose to avenge the murder of
his illustrious uncle and adoptive father.

[10] " Till you, traitors as you are, have added the slaughtering of me, another Cæsar, to that of Julius."

[11] *Strain* is *stock*, *lineage*, or *race ;* a common use of the word in Shakespeare's time. So in *King Henry V.*, ii. 4 : " He is bred out of that bloody
strain, that haunted us in our familiar paths."

[12] A peevish school-boy, joined with a masker and a reveller, and unworthy even of that honour. The more common meaning of *peevish* was
foolish.

[13] *Stomach* was often used for *appetite.* Here it means an appetite for
fighting, of course. See *Hamlet*, page 51, note 29.

The storm is up, and all is on the hazard.

    Bru. Ho, Lucilius! hark, a word with you.

    Lucil. My lord?   [BRUTUS *and* LUCILIUS *talk apart.*

    Cass. Messala,—

    Mes.   What says my General?

    Cass.   Messala,

This is my birth-day; as this very day

Was Cassius born.   Give me thy hand, Messala:

Be thou my witness that against my will,

As Pompey was,[14] I am compell'd to set

Upon one battle all our liberties.

You know that I held Epicurus strong,[15]

And his opinion: now I change my mind,

And partly credit things that do presage.

Coming from Sardis, on our foremost ensign

Two mighty eagles fell; and there they perch'd,

Gorging and feeding from our soldiers' hands;

Who to Philippi here consorted us:

This morning are they fled away and gone;[16]

---

[14] Alluding to the battle of Pharsalia, which took place in the year B.C. 48. Pompey was forced into that battle, against his better judgment, by the inexperienced and impatient men about him, who, inasmuch as they had more than twice Cæsar's number of troops, fancied they could easily crunch him up if they could but meet him. So they tried it, and he quickly crunched up them.

[15] "I was strongly attached to the doctrines of Epicurus." Plutarch has the following in reference to the ghosting of Brutus: "Cassius being in opinion an Epicurean, and reasoning thereon with Brutus, spake to him touching the vision thus: 'In our sect, Brutus, we have an opinion, that we do not always feel or see that which we suppose we do both see and feel, but that our senses, being credulous and therefore easily abused, (when they are idle and unoccupied in their own objects,) are induced to imagine they see and conjecture that which in truth they do not.'"

[16] When they raised their camp, there came two eagles that, flying with a marvellous force, lighted upon two of the foremost ensigns, and always

And in their steads do ravens, crows, and kites
Fly o'er our heads, and downward look on us,
As we were sickly prey :[17] their shadows seem
A canopy most fatal, under which
Our army lies, ready to give up the ghost.

    Mes. Believe not so.

    Cass.   I but believe it partly ;
For I am fresh of spirit, and resolved
To meet all perils very constantly.[18]

    Bru. Even so, Lucilius.

    Cass.   Now, most noble Brutus,
The gods to-day stand friendly, that we may,
Lovers in peace, lead on our days to age !

followed the soldiers, which gave them meat and fed them, until they came near to the city of Philippes ; and there, one day only before the battle, they both flew away. — PLUTARCH.

[17] And yet further, there were seen a marvellous number of fowls of prey, that feed upon dead carcases ; and bee-hives also were found where bees were gathered together in a certain place within the trenches of the camp ; the which place the soothsayers thought good to shut out of the precinct of the camp, for to take away the superstitious fear and mistrust men would have of it : the which began somewhat to alter Cassius's mind from Epicurus's opinions, and had put the soldiers also in a marvellous fear. — PLUTARCH.

[18] Touching Cassius, Messala reporteth that he supped by himself in his tent with a few of his friends, and that all supper-time he looked very sadly, and was full of thoughts, although it was against his nature ; and that after supper he took him by the hand, and, holding him fast, (in token of kindness, as his manner was,) told him in Greek : " Messala, I protest unto thee, and make thee my witness, that I am compelled against my mind and will (as Pompey the Great was) to jeopard the liberty of our country to the hazard of a battle. And yet we must be lively, and of good courage, considering our good fortune, whom we should wrong too much to mistrust her, although we follow evil counsel." Messala writeth, that Cassius having spoken these last words unto him, he bade him farewell, and willed him to come to supper to him the next night following, because it was his birth-day. — PLUTARCH.

But, since th' affairs of men rest still incertain,
Let's reason with [19] the worst that may befall.
If we do lose this battle, then is this
The very last time we shall speak together:
What are you then determinéd to do?

   Bru. Even by the rule of that philosophy
By which I did blame Cato for the death
Which he did give himself; — I know not how,
But I do find it cowardly and vile,
For fear of what might fall, so to prevent
The time of life; [20] — arming myself with patience
To stay the providence of some high powers
That govern us below.

   Cass.   Then, if we lose this battle,
You are contented to be led in triumph
Thorough the streets of Rome?

   Bru. No, Cassius, no: think not, thou noble Roman,
That ever Brutus will go bound to Rome;
He bears too great a mind.[21]   But this same day

   [19] To *reason with* here means to *talk* or *discourse about.* The use of to *reason* for to *converse* or *discourse* occurs repeatedly.

   [20] *Prevent* is here used in its literal sense of *anticipate.* — By *time* is meant the full time, the natural period. — To the understanding of this speech, it must be observed, that the *sense* of the words, " arming myself," &c., follows next after the words, "which he did give himself." — In this passage, Shakespeare was misled by an error in North's version of Plutarch, where we have *trust* instead of *trusted.* See the next note; where, instead of " Brutus answered him, being yet but a young man, — in the world: ' I trust,' " &c., it ought to be, " Brutus answered him : ' Being yet but a young man, — in the world, I trusted,' " &c.

   [21] The next morning, by break of day, the signal of battle was set out in Brutus's and Cassius's camp, which was an arming scarlet coat; and both the chieftains spake together in the midst of their armies. There Cassius began to speak first, and said : " The gods grant us, O Brutus, that this day we may win the field, and ever after to live all the rest of our life quietly one

Must end that work the Ides of March begun ;
And whether we shall meet again I know not.
Therefore our everlasting farewell take :
For ever, and for ever, farewell, Cassius !
If we do meet again, why, we shall smile ;
If not, why, then this parting was well made.

    Cass. For ever, and for ever, farewell, Brutus !
If we do meet again, we'll smile indeed ;
If not, 'tis true this parting was well made.

    Bru. Why, then lead on.   O, that a man might know
The end of this day's business ere it come !
But it sufficeth that the day will end,
And then the end is known. — Come, ho ! away ! [*Exeunt.*

SCENE II. — *The Same.   The Field of Battle.*

Alarum.   Enter BRUTUS *and* MESSALA.

    Bru. Ride, ride, Messala, ride, and give these bills
Unto the legions on the other side :[1]

with another.   But, sith the gods have so ordained it, that the greatest and
chiefest things amongst men are most uncertain, and that if the battle fall out
otherwise to-day than we wish or look for, we shall hardly meet again, what
art thou determined to do, to fly, or die ? " Brutus answered him, being yet
but a young man, and not over greatly experienced in the world, " I trust (I
know not how) a certain rule of philosophy, by the which I did greatly
blame and reprove Cato for killing himself, as being no lawful nor godly
act, touching the gods ; nor, concerning men, valiant ; not to give place and
yield to divine providence, and not constantly and patiently to take whatsoever it pleaseth him to send us, but to draw back and fly : but, being now in
the midst of the danger, I am of a contrary mind.   For, if it be not the will
of God that this battle fall out fortunate for us, I will look no more for hope,
neither seek to make any new supply for war again, but will rid me of this
miserable world, and content me with my fortune." — PLUTARCH.

[1] " The legions on the other side " are those commanded by Cassius ;
the left wing, in fact, of the joint army of Brutus and Cassius.   Brutus wants

Let them set on at once; for I perceive
But cold demeanor in Octavius' wing,
And sudden push gives them the overthrow.
Ride, ride, Messala: let them all come down.　　　[*Exeunt.*

SCENE III. — *Another Part of the Field.*

Alarum.　Enter CASSIUS *and* TITINIUS.

Cass.　O, look, Titinius, look, the villains fly!
Myself have to mine own turn'd enemy:
This ensign here of mine was turning back;
I slew the coward, and did take it from him.[2]
Tit.　O Cassius, Brutus gave the word too early;
Who, having some advantage on Octavius,
Took it too eagerly: his soldiers fell to spoil,
Whilst we by Antony are all enclosed.

Enter PINDARUS.

Pin.　Fly further off, my lord, fly further off;
Mark Antony is in your tents, my lord:
Fly, therefore, noble Cassius, fly far' off.
Cass.　This hill is far enough. — Look, look, Titinius;
Are those my tents where I perceive the fire?
Tit.　They are, my lord.
Cass.　　　　　　　　　　Titinius, if thou lovest me,
Mount thou my horse, and hide thy spurs in him,

Cassius to attack the enemy at the same time that he himself does.　In the
next scene, Messala and his escort are met by Titinius coming from Cassius.

2 *Ensign* was used, as it is still, either for the flag or for the bearer of it:
here it is used for both at once.　It was in killing the cowardly ensign that
Cassius "to his own turn'd enemy."

Till he have brought thee up to yonder troops,[3]
And here again; that I may rest assured
Whether yond troops are friend or enemy.

 Tit. I will be here again, even with a thought. [*Exit.*
 Cass. Go, Pindarus, get higher on that hill:[4]
My sight was ever thick: regard Titinius,
And tell me what thou notest about the field. —

         [PINDARUS *goes up.*

This day I breathèd first: time is come round,
And where I did begin, there shall I end;
My life is run his compass. — Sirrah, what news?
 Pin. [*Above.*] O my lord!
 Cass. What news?
 Pin. Titinius is enclosèd round about
With horsemen, that make to him on the spur:
Yet he spurs on. Now they are almost on him. —
Now, Titinius! — Now some 'light.[5] O, he 'lights too:
He's ta'en; [*Shout.*] and, hark! they shout for joy.
 Cass. Come down; behold no more. —
O, coward that I am, to live so long,
To see my best friend ta'en before my face! —

    PINDARUS *descends.*

Come hither, sirrah:
In Parthia did I take thee prisoner;
And then I swore thee, saving of thy life,
That whatsoever I did bid thee do,
Thou shouldst attempt it. Come now, keep thine oath;

---

 [3] "Yonder troops" are Messala and his escort coming from Brutus.

 [4] Cassius is now on a hill: he therefore means a hill somewhat *higher* than that he is on. — Cassius was, *in fact*, what we now call *near-sighted.*

 [5] Some *alight,* or *dismount.*

Now be a freeman ; and with this good sword,
That ran through Cæsar's bowels, search this bosom.
Stand not to answer : here, take thou the hilts ;[6]
And, when my face is cover'd, as 'tis now,
Guide thou the sword. — Cæsar, thou art revenged,
Even with the sword that kill'd thee.[7]　　　　　　　[*Dies*

　　Pin. So, I am free ; yet would not so have been,
Durst I have done my will. — O Cassius !
Far from this country Pindarus shall run,
Where never Roman shall take note of him.[8]　　　　[*Exit.*

---

　[6] *Hilts,* plural, for *hilt* was the common usage in the Poet's time. So too with *funerals,* later in this play.

　[7] It was a *dagger,* not a sword, that Cassius stabbed Cæsar with. But the same *weapon* is put for the same *owner;* a common figure of speech.

　[8] Cassius was at length compelled to fly, with a few about him, unto a little hill, from whence they might easily see what was done in all the plain : howbeit Cassius himself saw nothing, for his sight was very bad, saving that he saw (and yet with much ado) how the enemies spoiled his camp before his eyes. He also saw a great troop of horsemen, whom Brutus sent to aid him, and thought that they were his enemies that followed him ; but yet he sent Titinius, one of them that was with him, to go and know what they were. Brutus's horsemen saw him coming afar off, whom when they knew that he was one of Cassius's chiefest friends, they shouted out for joy ; and they that were familiarly acquainted with him lighted from their horses, and went and embraced him. The rest compassed him in round about on horseback, with songs of victory and great rushing of their harness, so that they made all the field ring again for joy. But this marred all. For Cassius, thinking indeed that Titinius was taken of the enemies, he then spake these words : " Desiring too much to live, I have lived to see one of my best friends taken, for my sake, before my face." After that, he got into a tent where nobody was, and took Pindarus with him, one of his bondsmen whom he reserved ever for such a pinch, since the cursed battle of the Parthians, where Crassus was slain, though he notwithstanding scaped from that overthrow : but then, casting his cloak over his head, and holding out his bare neck unto Pindarus, he gave him his head to be stricken off. So the head was found severed from the body : but after that time Pindarus was never seen more. — PLUTARCH.

Re-enter TITINIUS, *with* MESSALA.

Mess. It is but change,[9] Titinius; for Octavius
Is overthrown by noble Brutus' power,
As Cassius' legions are by Antony.

Tit. These tidings will well comfort Cassius.

Mes. Where did you leave him?

Tit.   All disconsolate,
With Pindarus his bondman, on this hill.

Mes. Is not that he that lies upon the ground?

Tit. He lies not like the living. O my heart!

Mes. Is not that he?

Tit.   No, this was he, Messala,
But Cassius is no more. — O setting Sun,
As in thy red rays thou dost sink to night,
So in his red blood Cassius' day is set;
The sun of Rome is set! Our day is gone;
Clouds, dews, and dangers come; our deeds are done!
Mistrust of my success hath done this deed.

Mes. Mistrust of good success hath done this deed.
O hateful Error, Melancholy's child!
Why dost thou show to the apt thoughts of men
The things that are not?[10] O Error, soon conceived,
Thou never comest unto a happy birth,
But kill'st the mother that engender'd thee!

Tit. What, Pindarus! where art thou, Pindarus?

Mes. Seek him, Titinius, whilst I go to meet
The noble Brutus, thrusting this report
Into his ears: I may say, thrusting it;

9 That is, *interchange* of victory and defeat.
10 Cassius is said to have been of a highly choleric or bilious temperament; as such, predisposed to melancholy, and hence apt to be taken with imaginary evils, or to construe things to the worst.

For piercing steel and darts envenoméd
Shall be as welcome to the ears of Brutus
As tidings of this sight.

    Tit.   Hie you, Messala,
And I will seek for Pindarus the while. —   [*Exit* MESSALA.
Why didst thou send me forth, brave Cassius?
Did I not meet thy friends? and did not they
Put on my brows this wreath of victory,
And bid me give it thee? Didst thou not hear their shouts?
Alas, thou hast misconstrued every thing!
But, hold thee, take this garland on thy brow;
Thy Brutus bid me give it thee, and I
Will do his bidding. — Brutus, come apace,
And see how I regarded Caius Cassius. —
By your leave, gods: this is a Roman's part:
Come, Cassius' sword, and find Titinius' heart.[11]   [*Dies.*

    Alarum. *Re-enter* MESSALA, *with* BRUTUS, *young* CATO,
        STRATO, VOLUMNIUS, *and* LUCILIUS.

    Bru. Where, where, Messala, doth his body lie?
    Mes. Lo, yonder, and Titinius mourning it.
    Bru. Titinius' face is upward.
    Cato.   He is slain.
    Bru. O Julius Cæsar, thou art mighty yet!
Thy spirit walks abroad, and turns our swords

---

11 By-and-by they knew the horsemen that came towards them, and might
see Titinius crowned with a garland of triumph, who came before with great
speed unto Cassius. But when he perceived, by the cries and tears of his
friends which tormented themselves, the misfortune that had chanced to
his captain Cassius by mistaking, he drew out his sword, cursing himself a
thousand times that he had tarried so long, and so slew himself presently
in the field. Brutus in the meantime came forward still, and understood
also that Cassius had been overthrown; but he knew nothing of his death
till he came very near to his camp. — PLUTARCH.

In our own proper entrails.[12]   [*Low alarums,*
    Cato.   Brave Titinius !
Look, whêr he have not crown'd dead Cassius !
    Bru. Are yet two Romans living such as these? —
Thou last of all the Romans, fare thee well !
It is impossible that ever Rome
Should breed thy fellow. — Friends, I owe more tears
To this dead man than you shall see me pay. —
I shall find time, Cassius, I shall find time. —
Come, therefore, and to Thassos send his body :
His funerals shall not be in our camp,
Lest it discomfort us.[13] — Lucilius, come ; —
And come, young Cato ; — let us to the field. —
Labeo and Flavius,[14] set our battles on : —
'Tis three o'clock ; and, Romans, yet ere night
We shall try fortune in a second fight.[15]   [*Exeunt.*

[12] Brutus here strikes the proper key-note of the play. The matter is well stated by Mr. Froude : "The murderers of Cæsar, and those who had either instigated them secretly or applauded them afterwards, were included in a proscription list, drawn by retributive justice on the model of Sulla's. Such of them as were in Italy were immediately killed. Those in the provinces, as if with the curse of Cain upon their heads, came one by one to miserable ends. In three years the tyrannicides of the Ides of March, with their aiders and abettors, were all dead ; some killed in battle, some in prison, some dying by their own hand."

[13] So when he was come thither, after he had lamented the death of Cassius, calling him the last of all the Romans, being unpossible that Rome should ever breed again so noble and valiant a man as he, he caused his body to be buried, and sent it to the city of Thassos, fearing lest his funerals within his camp should cause great disorder. — PLUTARCH.

[14] These two men are not named among the persons of the drama, because they speak nothing. Labeo was one of the stabbers of Cæsar ; and it is related that when he saw that all was lost, having dug his own grave, he enfranchised a slave, and then thrust a weapon into his hand to kill him.

[15] The Poet very judiciously represents both battles as occurring the same day. They were *in fact* separated by an interval of twenty days.

SCENE IV. — *Another Part of the Field.*

Alarum.   Enter, fighting, Soldiers *of both* Armies ; *then*
BRUTUS, *Young* CATO, LUCILIUS, *and Others.*

Bru. Yet, countrymen, O, yet hold up your heads !

Cato. What bastard doth not ?[1]   Who will go with me ?
I will proclaim my name about the field : —
I am the son of Marcus Cato, ho !
A foe to tyrants, and my country's friend ;
I am the son of Marcus Cato, ho !   [*Charges the* Enemy.

Bru. And I am Brutus, Marcus Brutus, I ;
Brutus, my country's friend ; know me for Brutus.

[*Exit, charging the* Enemy.   CATO *is
overpowered, and falls.*

Lucil. O young and noble Cato, art thou down ?
Why, now thou diest as bravely as Titinius ;
And mayst be honour'd, being Cato's son.[2]

1 Sold. Yield, or thou diest.

Lucil.   Only I yield to die :
There is so much that thou wilt kill me straight ;

[*Offering money.*

Kill Brutus, and be honour'd in his death.

1 Sold. We must not.   A noble prisoner !

2 Sold. Room, ho !   Tell Antony, Brutus is ta'en.

1 Sold. I'll tell the news.   Here comes the General. —

---

[1] Meaning, of course, "Who is such a bastard as not to do so ?" For
another like expression, see page 138, note 4.

[2] There was the son of Marcus Cato slain, valiantly fighting among the
lusty youth.   For notwithstanding that he was very weary and over-harried,
yet would he not therefore fly, but manfully fighting and laying about him,
telling aloud his name, and also his father's name, at length he was beaten
down amongst many other dead bodies of his enemies which he had slain
round about him. — PLUTARCH.

Enter ANTONY.

Brutus is ta'en, Brutus is ta'en, my lord.
  Ant. Where is he?
  Lucil. Safe, Antony; Brutus is safe enough:
I dare assure thee that no enemy
Shall ever take alive the noble Brutus:
The gods defend him from so great a shame!
When you do find him, or alive or dead,
He will be found like Brutus, like himself.
  Ant. This is not Brutus, friend; but, I assure you,
A prize no less in worth.   Keep this man safe,
Give him all kindness: I had rather have
Such men my friends than enemies.[3]   Go on,
And see whêr Brutus be alive or dead;
And bring us word unto Octavius' tent
How every thing is chanced.   [*Exeunt.*

[3] There was one of Brutus's friends called Lucilius, who seeing a troop
of barbarous men going right against Brutus, determined to stay them with
the hazard of his life, and, being left behind, told them that he was Brutus;
and, because they should believe him, he prayed them to bring him to Antonius, for he said he was afraid of Cæsar, and that he did trust Antonius
better.   These barbarous men, being very glad of this good hap, carried him
in the night, and sent some before unto Antonius to tell him of their coming.   He was marvellous glad of it, and went out to meet them that brought
him.   When they came near together, Antonius stayed awhile, bethinking
himself how he should use Brutus.   In the meantime Lucilius was brought
to him, who stoutly with a bold countenance said: "Antonius, I dare assure
thee, that no enemy hath taken or shall take Marcus Brutus alive, and I beseech God keep him from that fortune: for wheresoever he be found, alive
or dead, he will be found like himself.   And now, for myself, I am come
unto thee, having deceived these men of arms here, bearing them down that
I was Brutus, and do not refuse to suffer any torment thou wilt put me to."
Lucilius's words made them all amazed that heard him.   Antonius on the
other side, looking upon all them that had brought him, said unto them:
" My companions, I think ye are sorry you have failed of your purpose, and

SCENE V. — *Another Part of the Field.*

Enter BRUTUS, DARDANIUS, CLITUS, STRATO, *and* VOLUMNIUS.

Bru. Come, poor remains of friends, rest on this rock.

Cli. Statilius show'd the torch-light ; but, my lord,
He came not back : he is or ta'en or slain.[1]

Bru. Sit thee down, Clitus : slaying is the word ;
It is a deed in fashion.[2]   Hark thee, Clitus.   [*Whispering.*

---

that you think this man hath done you great wrong ; but I assure you, you
have taken a better booty than that you followed. For instead of an enemy
you have brought me a friend ; and, for my part, if you had brought me
Brutus alive, truly I cannot tell what I should have done to him. For I had
rather have such men my friends, as this man here, than mine enemies."
Then he embraced Lucilius, and at that time delivered him to one of his
friends in custody ; and Lucilius ever after served him faithfully, even to his
death. — PLUTARCH.

1 Brutus thought that there was no great number of men slain in battle ;
and, to know the truth of it, there was one called Statilius that promised to
go through his enemies, for otherwise it was impossible to go see their
camp ; and from thence, if all were well, that he would lift up a torch-light
in the air; and then return again with speed to him. The torch-light was
lift up as he had promised, for Statilius went thither. Now, Brutus seeing
Statilius tarry long after that, and that he came not again, he said, " If Statilius be alive, he will come again." But his evil fortune was such that, as
he came back, he lighted in his enemies' hands and was slain. — PLU-
TARCH.

2 The philosopher indeed renounced all confidence in his own principles.
He had adopted them from reading or imitation ; they were not the natural
growth of instinct or genuine reflection ; and, as may easily happen in such
a case, his faith in them failed when they were tested by adversity. As long
as there seemed a chance that the *godlike stroke* would be justified by success, Brutus claimed the glory of maintaining a righteous cause ; but, when
all hope fled, he could take leave of philosophy and life together, and ex-
claim, *I once dreamed that virtue was a thing ; I find her only a name, and
the mere slave of fortune.* He had blamed Cato for flying from misery by
self-murder ; but he learnt to justify the same desperate act when he con-
templated committing it himself. — MERIVALE.

Cli. What, I, my lord? No, not for all the world.

Bru. Peace then! no words.

Cli.   I'll rather kill myself.

Bru. Hark thee, Dardanius.   [*Whispers him.*

Dar.   Shall I do such a deed?

Cli. O Dardanius!

Dar. O Clitus!

Cli. What ill request did Brutus make to thee?

Dar. To kill him, Clitus. Look, he meditates.

Cli. Now is that noble vessel full of grief,
That it runs over even at his eyes.

Bru. Come hither, good Volumnius; list a word.

Vol. What says my lord?

Bru.   Why, this, Volumnius:
The ghost of Cæsar hath appear'd to me
Two several times by night; at Sardis once,
And, this last night, here in Philippi fields:
I know my hour is come.[3]

Vol.   Not so, my lord.

Bru. Nay, I am sure it is, Volumnius.
Thou see'st the world, Volumnius, how it goes;
Our enemies have beat us to the pit: [*Low alarums.*
It is more worthy to leap in ourselves
Than tarry till they push us. Good Volumnius,

---

[3] So the Poet read in Plutarch: "The second battle being at hand, this spirit appeared again unto him, but spake never a word. Thereupon Brutus, knowing that he should die, did put himself to all hazard in battle, but yet fighting could not be slain." — Merivale has a strong sentence on this point: "The legend that when preparing for the encounter with the triumvirs he was visited by the ghost of Cæsar, which summoned him to meet again at Philippi, marks the conviction of the ancients that in the crisis of his fate he was stung by guilty remorse, and haunted by the presentiment of final retribution."

Thou know'st that we two went to school together :
Even for that our love of old, I pr'ythee,
Hold thou my sword-hilts, whilst I run on it.

   Vol. That's not an office for a friend, my lord.

                                    [Alarums still.

   Cli. Fly, fly, my lord ! there is no tarrying here.

   Bru. Farewell to you ;—and you ;—and you, Volum-
      nius. —

Strato, thou hast been all this while asleep ;
Farewell to thee, too, Strato. — Countrymen,
My heart doth joy, that yet in all my life
I found no man but he was true to me.
I shall have glory by this losing day,
More than Octavius and Mark Antony
By their vile conquest shall attain unto.
So, fare you well at once ; for Brutus' tongue
Hath almost ended his life's history :
Night hangs upon mine eyes ; my bones would rest,
That have but labour'd to attain this hour.

                    [Alarums.   Cry within, Fly, fly, fly !

   Cli. Fly, my lord, fly !

   Bru.   Hence ! I will follow. —

               [Exeunt CLIT., DARDAN., *and* VOLUM.

I pr'ythee, Strato, stay thou by thy lord :
Thou art a fellow of a good respect ; [4]
Thy life hath had some smack of honour in it :
Hold, then, my sword, and turn away thy face,
While I do run upon it.   Wilt thou, Strato ?

   Stra. Give me your hand first : fare you well, my lord.

   Bru. Farewell, good Strato. — Cæsar, now be still :

---

[4] A fellow *well esteemed*, or of good *reputation*.   See page 48, note **17**.

I kill'd not thee with half so good a will.[5]

> [*He runs on his sword, and dies.*

Alarum.   Retreat.   Enter OCTAVIUS, ANTONY, MESSALA, LU-
CILIUS, *and* Army.

  Oct. What man is that?

  Mes. My master's man. — Strato, where is thy master?

  Stra. Free from the bondage you are in, Messala:
The conquerors can but make a fire of him;
For Brutus only overcame himself,
And no man else hath honour by his death.

  Lucil. So Brutus should be found. — I thank thee, Brutus,

---

[5] Now the night being far spent, Brutus as he sat bowed towards Clitus, one of his men, and told him somewhat in his ear: the other answered him not, but fell a-weeping. Thereupon he proved Dardanius, and said somewhat also to him: at length he came to Volumnius himself, and, speaking to him in Greek, prayed him for the studies' sake which brought them acquainted together, that he would help him to put his hand to his sword, to thrust it in him to kill him. Volumnius denied his request, and so did many others; and, amongst the rest, one of them said, there was no tarrying for them there, but that they must needs fly. Then Brutus, rising up, "We must fly indeed," said he, "but it must be with our hands, not with our feet." Then, taking every man by the hand, he said these words unto them with a cheerful countenance: "It rejoiceth my heart, that not one of my friends hath failed me at my need, and I do not complain of my fortune, but only for my country's sake: for, as for me, I think myself happier than they that have overcome, considering that I leave a perpetual fame of virtue and honesty, the which our enemies the conquerors shall never attain unto by force or money; neither can let their posterity to say that they, being naughty and unjust men, have slain good men, to usurp tyrannical power not pertaining to them." Having so said, he prayed every man to shift for himself, and then he went a little aside with two or three only, among the which Strato was one, with whom he came first acquainted by the study of rhetoric. He came as near him as he could, and taking his sword by the hilt with both his hands, and falling down upon the point of it, ran himself through. Others say that not he, but Strato, at his request, held the sword in his hand, and turned his head aside, and that Brutus fell down upon it, and so ran himself through, and died presently. — PLUTARCH.

That thou hast proved Lucilius' saying true.

   Oct. All that served Brutus, I will entertain them.[6] —
Fellow, wilt thou bestow thy time with me?

   Stra. Ay, if Messala will prefer me to you.[7]

   Oct. Do so, good Messala.

   Mes. How died my master, Strato?

   Stra. I held the sword, and he did run on it.

   Mes. Octavius, then take him to follow thee,
That did the latest service to my master.

   Ant. This was the noblest Roman of them all:
All the conspirators, save only he,
Did that they did in envy of great Cæsar;
He only, in a general-honest thought
And common good to all,[8] made one of them.
His life was gentle; and the elements
So mix'd in him,[9] that Nature might stand up
And say to all the world, *This was a man!*

   Oct. According to his virtue let us use him,
With all respect and rites of burial.
Within my tent his bones to-night shall lie,
Most like a soldier, order'd honourably. —
So, call the field to rest; and let's away,
To part the glories of this happy day.   *[Exeunt.*

   [6] "I will take them into my service." So in *The Two Gentlemen,* ii. 4:
"Sweet lady, *entertain* him for your servant."

   [7] *Prefer* was a common term for *recommending* a servant.

   [8] The force of *in* is, properly, continued over *common good.*

   [9] Referring to the old doctrine of the four elements, as they were called,
earth, water, air, and fire, the right mixing and tempering of which was supposed to be the principle of all excellence in Nature. The Poet has a number of allusions to the doctrine, which was a commonplace of the time. The
sense of the word *elements* has so changed as to make the passage just as
true to the ideas of our time, as it was to those of three hundred years ago.
A rather curious fact.

THE FUNERAL OF CÆSAR.*

THE Dictator had bequeathed to each citizen the sum of three hundred sesterces, or rather less than three pounds sterling. The money itself, indeed, was not forthcoming; for Antonius had already disposed of the whole treasure which had fallen into his hands. But Octavius had not yet arrived to discharge his patron's legacies; many formalities and some chances lay between the public avowal of these generous intentions and the claim for their actual fulfilment; and Antonius in the meantime might turn to his own account the grateful acknowledgment of the people for a largess they might never be destined to enjoy. The bare recital of Cæsar's testament operated on their feelings most favourably to his interests. Now for the first time they were fully roused to a sense of their benefactor's wrongs. Now for the first time the black ingratitude of Decimus and the others, his confidants and his assassins, stood revealed in its hideous deformity. The sense of personal loss stifled every

---

* The paragraphs that follow under this heading are from Merivale's *History of the Romans under the Empire*, Chapter xxiii. Taken all together, they form, to my judgment, one of the finest pieces of historical portraiture that I know of in the language. And the passage illustrates so happily the most interesting scene of the foregoing drama, that no apology seems needful for reproducing it here. I have often read it, with good effect, to my own Shakespeare classes in connection with that scene.

specious argument that could be advanced to extenuate the crime. The vindication of the laws, the assertion of liberty, the overthrow of a tyrant and a dynasty of tyrants, all sank at once before the paramount iniquity of destroying the only substantial benefactor the Roman people had ever had. Many a magistrate or conqueror indeed had lavished shows and festivals upon them ; the city owed its noblest ornaments to the rivalry of suitors for popularity ; but these were candidates for honours and distinctions, and had all a personal object to serve ; while the bequest of the murdered Julius was deemed an act of pure generosity, for the dead can have no selfish interests.

The heralds proclaimed throughout the city the appointed place and hour of the obsequies. A funeral pyre was constructed in the Field of Mars, close to the spot where lay the ashes of Julia ; for the laws forbade cremation within the walls ; and the laws, enacted for purposes of health, were reinforced by feelings of superstition. But the funeral oration was to be pronounced in the Forum, and a temporary chapel, open on every side, modelled, it is said, after the temple of Venus the Ancestress, was erected before the rostra, and gorgeously gilded, for the reception of the body. The bier was a couch inlaid with ivory, and strewn with vestments of gold and purple. At its head was suspended, in the fashion of a warrior's trophy, the toga in which the Dictator had been slain, pierced through and through by the assassins' daggers. Calpurnius Piso walked at the head of the procession, as chief mourner ; the body was borne by the highest magistrates and most dignified personages of the State ; the people were invited to make oblations for the pyre, of garments, arms, trinkets, and spices. So great was the concourse of the offerers, that the order in which they were appointed to present themselves could not be preserved, but every one was allowed to approach the spot by whatever route he chose from every corner of the city. When the mangled remains were deposited in their place, they were concealed from the gaze of the multitude; but in their stead a waxen effigy was raised aloft, and turned about by machinery in every direction; and the people could distinctly mark the three-and-twenty wounds represented faithfully upon it. Dramatic shows formed, as usual, a part of the ceremony. Passages from the *Electra* of Atillius, and the *Contest for the Arms of Achilles*, a celebrated piece of Pacuvius, were enacted on the occasion. The murder of Agamemnon, and the requital of Ajax, who complained that in saving the Greeks he had saved his own assassins, furnished pungent allusions to the circumstances of the time, and moved the sensibilities of an inflammable populace.

While the feelings of the citizens were thus melting with compassion or glowing with resentment, Antonius came forward, as the first magistrate of the republic, to deliver the funeral eulogy due to the mighty dead. Historians and poets have felt the intense interest of the position he at that moment occupied, and have vied with each other in delineating with the nicest touches the adroitness he displayed in guiding the passions of his audience. Suetonius indeed asserts that he added few words of his own to the bare recital of the decrees of the Senate, by which every honour, human and divine, had been heaped upon Cæsar, and of the oath by which his destined assassins had bound themselves to his defence. But Cicero tells a different story. He speaks with bitter indignation of the praises, the commiseration, and the inflammatory appeals, which he interwove with the address. With such contemporary authority before us, we may believe that the speech reported by Appian is no rhetorical fiction, but a fair representation, both in manner and substance, of the actual harangue. The most exquisite scene in the truest of all Shakespeare's historical delineations adds little, except the charm of verse and the vividness of dramatic action, to the graphic painting of the original record.

This famous speech was in fact a consummate piece of dramatic art. The eloquence of Antonius was less moving than the gestures which enforced it, and the accessory circumstances which he enlisted to plead on his behalf. He addressed himself to the eyes, no less than to the ears of his audience. He disclaimed the position of a panegyrist: his friendship with the deceased might render his testimony suspected. He was, indeed, unworthy to praise Cæsar: the voice of the people alone could pronounce his befitting eulogy. He produced the Acts of the Senate, and of the faction by whose hands Cæsar had fallen, as the vouchers of his assertions. These he recited with a voice tremulous with grief, and a countenance struggling with emotions. He read the decrees which had within a twelvemonth heaped honours upon Cæsar, and which declared his person inviolable, his authority supreme, and himself the chief and father of his country. Were these honours excessive or dangerous to the State, the Senate had bestowed them: did they even trench upon the attributes of the gods, the pontiffs had sanctioned them. And when he came to the words *consecrated, inviolable, father of his country*, the orator pointed with artful irony to the bleeding and lifeless corpse, which neither laws nor oaths had shielded from outrage. He paused, and the dramatic chorus sent forth some ancient wail, such as ages before had been consecrated to the sorrows of heroes, who like Cæsar had been kings of men, and of Houses which like the Julian had sprung from gods and goddesses.

Then, from these examples of high fortune and its tragic issues, he passed on to recite the solemn oath by which the Senate, the nobles, and among them the conspirators themselves, had devoted their hearts and hands to their hero's defence ; and thereupon, turning with glowing emotion towards the temple of Jupiter, conspicuous on the Capitol, he exclaimed : "And I, for my part, am prepared to maintain my vow, to avenge the victim I could not save." Such words from the chief magistrate of the State were deeply impressive. The Senators scowled and murmured. Antonius pretended to check his impetuosity and address himself to soothing their alarm. After all, he said, it was not the work of men, it was the judgment of the gods. Cæsar was too great, too noble, too far above the race of men, too nigh to the nature of the immortals, to be overthrown by any power but that of divinity itself. " Let us bow," he exclaimed, " to the stroke as mortal men. Let us bury the past in oblivion. Let us bear away these venerable remains to the abodes of the blessed, with due lamentations and deserved eulogies ! "

With these words the consummate actor girt his robes closely around him, and striding to the bier, with his head inclined before it, muttered a hymn to the body, as to the image of a god. In rapid verse or solemn modulated prose he chanted the mighty deeds and glories of the deceased, the trophies he had won, the triumphs he had led, the riches he had poured into the treasury. "Thou, Cæsar, alone wast never worsted in battle. Thou alone hast avenged our defeats and wiped away our disgraces. By thee the insults of three hundred years stand requited. Before thee has fallen the hereditary foe who burned the city of our fathers." So did the Potitii and Pinarii recite their hymns to Hercules : so did the frantic hierophant sing the praises of Apollo. The flamen of Julius seemed instinct with the inspiration of the altar and the tripod, while he breathed the fanatic devotion of the ancient faith.

The blood-smeared image was turned this way and that for all eyes to gaze upon ; and, as it seemed to writhe in the agonies of death, the groans of men and the shrieks of women drowned the plaintive accents of the speaker. Suddenly Antonius raised the mangled garment which hung over the body itself, and waving it before the people disclosed the rents of the murderers' daggers. The excitement of the populace now became uncontrollable. Religious enthusiasm fanned the flame of personal sympathy. They forbade the body to be carried to the Field of Mars for cremation. Some pointed to the temple of Jupiter, where the effigy of the demigod had been enthroned in front of the deity himself, and demanded that it should be burnt in the holy shrine, and its ashes deposited among its kindred divinities. The priests stepped forward to avert this profanation ; and it was then proposed to consume the body in the Pompeian Curia, whence the mighty spirit had winged its flight to the celestial mansions.

Meanwhile chairs, benches, and tables had been snatched from the adjacent buildings, a heap of fuel was raised before the door of the pontifical mansion in the Forum, and the body snatched by tumultuary hands was cast upon it in a frenzy of excitement. Two young men, girt with swords, and javelin in hand, were seen to apply the torch. Such a vision had appeared in ancient times in the heat of battle. Castor and Pollux, it was believed, had descended more than once in human form to save the republic. A divine sanction was thus given to the deed : every scruple was overruled ;

and it was resolved to consume the hero's remains in the heart of his own city. The people continued to pile up branches and brushwood; the musicians and players added their costly garments to the heap, the veterans their arms, the matrons their ornaments; even the trinkets which adorned the children's frocks were torn off, and offered in the blazing conflagration.

Cæsar was beloved by the Romans : he was not less dear to the foreigners who owed so much to his ascendency, and had anticipated so much more. Gauls, Iberians, Africans, and Orientals, crowded in successive groups around the pyre, and gave vent to the sense of their common misfortune. Among them the Jews were eminently conspicuous. Cæsar was the only Roman who had respected their feelings, and assured them of his sympathy. Many of this people continued for several nights to assemble with sorrow and resentment on the spot, and uttered another funeral dirge over the blighted hopes of their nation.

Cæsar and the Conspirators.*

SIXTY Senators, in all, were parties to the immediate conspiracy. Of these, nine tenths were members of the old faction whom Cæsar had pardoned, and who, of all his acts, resented most that he

* The following pages are from the last three chapters of Mr. J. A. Froude's new book entitled *Cæsar: A Sketch.* I am far from concurring always, or even generally, in the accomplished author's opinions; and his style, though eminently readable, lacks, I must think, something of the calmness and candour proper to historic writing : but what he says of Cæsar and his stabbers is, to my sense, no less true and just in matter than fresh, vigorous, and tasteful in manner. The surpassing greatness both of Cæsar himself and of the space he occupies in history will, I trust, be held a sufficient reason for giving the matter a place in this volume.

had been able to pardon them. Their motives were the ambition
of their order and personal hatred of Cæsar: but they persuaded
themselves that they were animated by patriotism; and as, in
their hands, the Republic had been a mockery of liberty, so they
aimed at restoring it by a mock tyrannicide. Their oaths and
their professions were nothing to them. If they were entitled to
kill Cæsar, they were entitled equally to deceive him. No stronger
evidence is needed of the demoralization of the Roman Senate
than the completeness with which they were able to disguise from
themselves the baseness of their treachery. One man only they
were able to attract into coöperation who had a reputation for
honesty, and could be conceived, without absurdity, to be animated by a disinterested purpose.

Marcus Brutus was the son of Cato's sister Servilia; and
although, under the influence of his uncle, he had taken the Senate's side in the war, he had accepted afterwards not pardon only
from Cæsar, but favours of many kinds, for which he had pro-
fessed, and probably felt, some real gratitude. He had married
Cato's daughter, Portia, and, on Cato's death had published a
eulogy upon him. Cæsar left him free to think and write what
he pleased. He had made him Prætor; he had nominated him
to the governorship of Macedonia. Brutus was perhaps the only
member of the senatorial party in whom Cæsar felt genuine confidence. His known integrity, and Cæsar's acknowledged regard
for him made his accession to the conspiracy an object of particular importance. The name of Brutus would be a guaranty to
the people of rectitude of intention. Brutus, as the world went,
was of more than average honesty. He had sworn to be faithful
to Cæsar, as the rest had sworn; and an oath with him was not
a thing to be emotionalized away: but he was a fanatical republican, a man of gloomy habits, given to dreams and omens, and
easily liable to be influenced by appeals to visionary feelings.
Caius Cassius, his brother-in-law, was employed to work upon
him. Cassius, too, was Prætor that year, having been also nominated to office by Cæsar. He knew Brutus, he knew where and
how to move him. He reminded him of the great traditions of

his name. A Brutus had delivered Rome from the Tarquins. The blood of a Brutus was consecrated to liberty. This, too, was mockery: Brutus, who expelled the Tarquins, had put his sons to death, and died childless: Marcus Brutus came of good plebeian family, with no glories of tyrannicide about them; but the imaginary genealogy suited well with the spurious heroics which veiled the motives of Cæsar's murderers.

Brutus, once wrought upon, became with Cassius the most ardent in the cause, which assumed the aspect to him of a sacred duty. Behind them were the crowd of Senators of the familiar faction, and others worse than they, who had not even the excuse of having been partisans of the beaten cause; men who had fought at Cæsar's side till the war was over, and believed, like Labienus, that to them Cæsar owed his fortune. One of these was Trebonius, who had misbehaved himself in Spain, and was smarting under the recollection of his own failures. Trebonius had been named by Cæsar for a future consulship; but a distant reward was too little for him. Another and yet a baser traitor was Decimus Brutus, whom Cæsar valued and trusted beyond all his officers; whom he had selected as guardian for Octavius, and had noticed, as was seen afterwards, with special affection in his will. The services of these men were invaluable to the conspirators on account of their influence with the army. Decimus Brutus, like Labienus, had enriched himself in Cæsar's campaigns, and had amassed near half a million of English money.

So composed was this memorable band, to whom was to fall the bad distinction of completing the ruin of the senatorial rule. Cæsar would have spared something of it; enough, perhaps, to have thrown up shoots again as soon as he had himself passed away in the common course of nature. By combining in a focus the most hateful characteristics of the order, by revolting the moral instincts of mankind by ingratitude and treachery, they stripped their cause of the false glamour which they hoped to throw over it. The profligacy and avarice, the cynical disregard of obligation, which had marked the Senate's supremacy for a century, had exhibited abundantly their unfitness for the high functions which had descended to them; but custom, and natural tenderness for a form of government, the past history of which had been so glorious, might have continued still to shield them from the penalty of their iniquities. The murder of Cæsar filled the measure of their crimes, and gave the last and necessary impulse to the closing act of the revolution.

Cæsar was dead. But Cæsar still lived. "It was not possible that the grave should hold him." The people said that he was a god, and had gone back to Heaven, where his star had been seen ascending; his spirit remained on Earth, and the vain blows of the assassins had been but "malicious mockery." "We have killed the king," exclaimed Cicero in the bitterness of his disenchantment, "but the kingdom is with us still": "we have taken away the tyrant; the tyranny survives."

Cæsar had not overthrown the oligarchy: their own incapacity, their own selfishness, their own baseness, had overthrown them. Cæsar had been but the reluctant instrument of the Power which metes out to men the inevitable penalties of their own misdeeds. They had dreamt that the Constitution was a living force which would revive of itself as soon as its enemy was gone. They did not know that it was dead already, and that they had themselves destroyed it. The Constitution was but an agreement by which the Roman people had consented to abide for their common good. It had ceased to be for the common good. The experience of fifty miserable years had proved that it meant the supremacy of the rich, maintained by the bought votes of demoralized electors. The soil of Italy, the industry and happiness of tens of millions of mankind, from the Rhine to the Euphrates, had been the spoil of five hundred families and their relatives and dependents, of men whose occupation was luxury, and whose appetites were for monstrous pleasures. The self-respect of reasonable men could no longer tolerate such a rule in Italy or out of it.

In killing Cæsar the Optimates had been as foolish as they were treacherous; for Cæsar's efforts had been to reform the Constitution, not to abolish it. The Civil War had risen from their dread of his second consulship, which they had feared would make an end of their corruptions; and that the Constitution should be purged of the poison in its veins, was the sole condition on which its continuance was possible. The obstinacy, the ferocity, the treachery of the aristocracy had compelled Cæsar to crush them; and the more desperate their struggles, the more absolute the necessity became. But he alone could have restored as much of popular liberty as was consistent with the responsibilities of such a government as the Empire required. In Cæsar alone were combined the intellect and the power necessary for such a work: they had killed him, and in doing so had passed final sentence on themselves. Not as realities any more, but as harmless phantoms, the forms of the old Republic were henceforth to persist.

Personal Traits of Cæsar.

In person Cæsar was tall and slight. His features were more refined than was usual in Roman faces; the forehead was wide and high, the nose large and thin, the lips full, the eyes dark gray like an eagle's, the neck extremely thick and sinewy. His complexion was pale. His beard and moustache were kept carefully shaved. His hair was short and naturally scanty, falling off towards the end of his life, and leaving him partially bald. His voice, especially when he spoke in public, was high and shrill. His health was uniformly strong until his last year, when he became subject to epileptic fits. He was a great bather, and scrupulously clean in all his habits; abstemious in his food, and careless in what it consisted; rarely or never touching wine, and noting sobriety as the highest of qualities, when describing any new people. He was an athlete in early life, admirable in all manly exercises, and especially in riding. In Gaul he rode a remarkable horse, which he had bred himself, and which would let no one but Cæsar mount him. From his boyhood it was observed that he was the truest of friends, that he avoided quarrels, and was most easily appeased when offended. In manner he was quiet and gentlemanlike, with the natural courtesy of high breeding. On an occasion when he was dining somewhere, the other guests found the oil too rancid for them: Cæsar took it without remark, to spare his entertainer's feelings. When on a journey through a forest with his friend Oppius, he came one night to a hut where there was a single bed. Oppius being unwell, Cæsar gave it up to him, and slept on the ground.

Cæsar as a Statesman.

Like Cicero, Cæsar entered public life at the bar. He belonged by birth to the popular party, but he showed no disposition, like the Gracchi, to plunge into political agitation. His aims were practical. He made war only upon injustice and oppression; and, when he commenced as a pleader, he was noted for the energy with which he protected a client whom he believed to have been wronged. When he rose into the Senate, his powers as a speaker became strikingly remarkable. Cicero, who often heard him, and was not a favourable judge, said that there was a pregnancy in his sentences and a dignity in his manner which no orator in Rome could approach. But he never spoke to court popularity: his aim from first to last was better government, the prevention of bribery and extortion, and the distribution among deserving citizens of some portion of the public land which the rich were stealing. The Julian laws, which excited the indignation of the aristocracy, had no other objects than these; and had they been observed they would have saved the Constitution. The purpose of government he conceived to be the execution of justice; and a constitutional liberty under which justice was made impossible did not appear to him to be liberty at all.

Cæsar, it was observed, when any thing was to be done, selected the man who was best able to do it, not caring particularly who or what he might be in other respects. To this faculty of discerning and choosing fit persons to execute his orders may be ascribed the extraordinary success of his own provincial administration, the enthusiasm which was felt for him in the North of

Italy, and the perfect quiet of Gaul after the completion of the conquest. Cæsar did not crush the Gauls under the weight of Italy. He took the best of them into the Roman service, promoted them, led them to associate the interests of the Empire with their personal advancement and the prosperity of their own people. No act of Cæsar's showed more sagacity than the introduction of Gallic nobles into the Senate; none was more bitter to the Scipios and Metelli, who were compelled to share their august privileges with these despised barbarians.

Cæsar in War.

It was by accident that Cæsar took up the profession of a soldier; yet perhaps no commander who ever lived showed greater military genius. The conquest of Gaul was effected by a force numerically insignificant, which was worked with the precision of a machine. The variety of uses to which it was capable of being turned implied, in the first place, extraordinary forethought in the selection of materials. Men whose nominal duty was merely to fight were engineers, architects, mechanics of the highest order. In a few hours they could extemporize an impregnable fortress on an open hillside. They bridged the Rhine in a week. They built a fleet in a month. The legions at Alesia held twice their number pinned within their works, while they kept at bay the whole force of insurgent Gaul, entirely by scientific superiority.

The machine, which was thus perfect, was composed of human beings who required supplies of tools, and arms, and clothes, and food, and shelter; and for all these it depended on the forethought of its commander. Maps there were none. Countries entirely unknown had to be surveyed; routes had to be laid out; the depths and courses of rivers, the character of mountain passes, had all to be ascertained. Allies had to be found among tribes as yet unheard of. Countless contingent difficulties had to be provided for, many of which must necessarily arise, though the exact nature of them could not be anticipated.

When room for accidents is left open, accidents do not fail to be heard of. But Cæsar was never defeated when personally present, save once at Gergovia, and once at Durazzo: the failure at Gergovia was caused by the revolt of the Ædui; and the manner in which the failure at Durazzo was retrieved showed Cæsar's greatness more than the most brilliant of his victories. He was rash, but with a calculated rashness, which the event never failed to justify. His greatest successes were due to the rapidity of his movements, which brought him on the enemy before they heard of his approach. He travelled sometimes a hundred miles a-day, reading or writing in his carriage, through countries without roads, and crossing rivers without bridges. No obstacle stopped him when he had a definite end in view. In battle he sometimes rode; but he was more often on foot, bareheaded, and in a conspicuous dress, that he might be seen and recognized. Again and again by his own efforts he recovered a day that was half lost. He once seized a panic-stricken standard-bearer, turned him round, and told him that he had mistaken the direction of the enemy. He never misled his army as to an enemy's strength; or, if he misstated their numbers, it was only to exaggerate.

Yet he was singularly careful of his soldiers. He allowed his legions rest, though he allowed none to himself. He rarely fought a battle at a disadvantage. He never exposed his men to unnecessary danger; and the loss by wear and tear in the campaigns in Gaul was exceptionally and even astonishingly slight. When a gallant action was performed, he knew by whom it had been done; and every soldier, however humble, might feel assured that if he deserved praise he would have it. The army was Cæsar's family. When Sabinus was cut off, he allowed his beard to grow, and he did not shave it till the disaster was avenged. If Quintus Cicero had been his own child, he could not have run greater personal risk to save him when shut up at Charleroy. In discipline he was lenient to ordinary faults, and not careful to make curious inquiries into such things. He liked his men to enjoy themselves. Military mistakes in his officers, too, he always endeavoured to excuse, never blaming them for misfortunes, unless there had been a defect of courage as well as judgment. Mutiny and desertion only he never overlooked. And thus no general was ever more loved by, or had greater power over, the army which served under him.

His leniency to the Pompeian faction may have been politic, but it arose also from the disposition of the man. Cruelty originates in fear, and Cæsar was too indifferent to death to fear any thing. So far as his public action was concerned, he betrayed no passion save hatred of injustice; and he moved through life calm and irresistible, like a force of Nature.

Cæsar as an Author.

Cicero has said of Cæsar's oratory, that he surpassed those who practised no other art. His praise of him as a man of letters is yet more delicately and gracefully emphatic. Most of his writings are lost; but there remain seven books of Commentaries on the wars in Gaul, and three books upon the Civil War. Of these it was that Cicero said, in an admirable image, that fools might think to improve on them, but that no wise man would try it; they were bare of ornament, the dress of style dispensed with, like an undraped human figure perfect in all its lines, as Nature made it. In his composition, as in his actions, Cæsar is entirely simple. He indulges in no images, no laboured descriptions, no conventional reflections. His art is unconscious, as the highest art always is. The actual fact of things stands out as it really was, not as mechanically photographed, but interpreted by the calmest intelligence, and described with unexaggerated feeling. No military narrative has approached the excellence of the history of the war in Gaul. Nothing is written down which could be dispensed with; nothing important is left untold; while the incidents themselves are set off by delicate and just observations on human character.

The books on the Civil War have the same simplicity and clearness, but a vein runs through them of strong if subdued emotion. They contain the history of a great revolution related by the principal actor in it; but no effort can be traced to set his own side in a favourable light, or to abuse or depreciate his adversaries. Cæsar does not exult over his triumphs or parade the honesty of his motives. The facts are left to tell their own story; and the gallantry and endurance of his own troops are not related with more feeling than the contrast of the confident hopes of the patrician leaders at Pharsalia and the luxury of their camp with the overwhelming disaster which fell upon them. About himself and his own exploits there is not one word of self-complacency or self-admiration. In his writings, as in his life, Cæsar is always the same, — direct, straightforward, unmoved save by occasional tenderness, describing with unconscious simplicity how the work which had been forced upon him was accomplished. He wrote with extreme rapidity in the intervals of other labour; yet there is not a word misplaced, not a sign of haste anywhere, save that the conclusion of the Gallic war was left to be supplied by a weaker hand.

CRITICAL NOTES.

ACT I., SCENE I.

Page 39. *Enter* FLAVIUS, MARULLUS, &c. — In the original, the latter of these names is printed *Murellus*. So all through the play except in one instance, where it is *Murrellus*.

P. 40. *Mar.* **What trade, thou knave? thou naughty knave, what trade?** — The original prefixes "*Fla.*" to this speech; but the next two speeches prove, beyond question, that it belongs to Marullus. Corrected by Capell.

P. 41. I meddle with no tradesman's matters, nor women's matters, but with awl. — The original has "but *withal.*" Of course a quibble is intended between *all* and *awl;* and it is not clear which form ought to be used. As the quibble is addressed to the ear, it matters little. — Some have found fault with *tradesman's,* and Farmer proposed to read "no *trade,* — *man's* matters, nor woman's." Walker observes, "Surely this is at least a step to the right reading."

ACT I., SCENE II.

P. 44. Stand you directly in Antonius' way. — Here, and generally, the name is printed *Antonio* in the original. And so with several other names, *Octavio, Flavio,* and *Claudio.* Perhaps this grew, as Steevens thought, from the players being more used to Italian than to Roman terminations.

P. 47. **No, Cassius; for the eye sees not itself**
     But by reflection from some other thing. — The original
reads "by reflection, *by* some other *things*." Here *by* was doubtless
repeated by mistake ; and singulars and plurals were very often confounded. The first of these corrections was made by Pope ; the other,
by Walker.

P. 48. **That you have no such mirror as will turn**
     Your hidden worthiness into your eye. — The old text has
mirrors instead of *mirror*. Corrected by Walker.

P. 48. **Were I a common laugher, or did use**
     To stale with ordinary oaths my love
     To every new protester. — So Pope. Instead of *laugher*,
the original has *Laughter ;* which, after all, may possibly be right, in
the sense of *laughingstock*. Some one has proposed "a common
lover"; and so, I have hardly any doubt, we ought to read. This
would make *common* emphatic, and give it the sense of *indiscriminate*
or *promiscuous ;* which quite accords with the context.

P. 49. **Set honour in one eye, and death i' the other,**
     And I will look on death indifferently. — So Theobald and
Warburton. In the second of these lines, the original has *both* instead
of *death*. With *both*, the paralogism is surely too glaring, even for so
loose-knit a genius as Brutus.

P. 53. **When could they say, till now, that talk'd of Rome,**
     That her wide walls encompass'd but one man? — The
original has *walkes* instead of *walls*. Perhaps the error grew from
talk'd in the preceding line. Corrected by Rowe.

P. 55. **As we have seen him in the Capitol,**
     Being cross'd in conference by some Senator. — So Walk-
er. The original has *Senators*.

P. 60. **Ay, if I be alive, and your mind hold, and your dinner**
worth the eating. — Walker says, "Surely, 'and *my* mind hold.'
Your is absurd." Perhaps so; but I do not quite see it.

ACT I., SCENE III.

P. 63. **A common slave — you'd know him well by sight —**
Held up his left hand, &c. — The original reads "*you* know
him," &c. The correction is proposed by Dyce. The propriety of it
is, I think, evident. See foot-note 6.

P. 63. **Against the Capitol I met a lion,**
Who glared upon me, &c. — The original has *glaz'd* instead
of *glared*. Hardly worth noting, perhaps.

P. 64.   **When these prodigies**
Do so conjointly meet, let not men say,
These are their reasons; they are natural. — Collier's second folio changes *reasons* to *seasons*. Upon this reading Professor
Craik comments thus: "*This is their season* might have been conceiv-
able; but who ever heard it remarked of any description of phenom-
ena that *these are their seasons*." Nevertheless I am pretty sure that
similar phrases are current in common speech. And if any one were
to say, "These parts of the year," or, "these months of Spring,
are just the *times*," or "the *seasons* for such storms," where would be
the absurdity of it? Besides, I do not see but that strict propriety of
speech requires *this is their reason*, as much as *this is their season*. So
I am apt to think that *seasons* is the right reading. See, however, foot-
note 11.

P. 66.   **You look pale, and gaze,**
And put on fear, and case yourself in wonder, &c. — The
old text has *cast* instead of *case*. The correction occurred indepen-
dently to Mr. Swynfen Jervis and Mr. W. W. Williams, and is certainly
favoured by the words *put on fear*. See foot-note 18.

P. 66. **Why old men fool, and children calculate.** — The original reads "Why Old men, Fooles, and Children calculate." This
makes the sense incoherent. The reading here adopted is coherent,
and gives the right sense, — that old men in being foolish, and children
in being considerate, are acting as much against nature as the fires and

ghosts, the birds and beasts, are in what has just been related of them. The correction was proposed by Mitford. Lettsom says, "Read 'old men fool,' if this has not been noticed before."

P. 67. **To make them instruments of fear and warning**
        Unto some monstrous state.   Now could I, Casca,
        Name thee a man most like this dreadful night, &c. — So Capell.   The original reads "Name *to* thee a man."

P. 70. **And the complexion of the element**
        Is favour'd like the work we have in hand,
        Most bloody-fiery and most terrible. — In the second of these lines, the original has "*Is Favors*, like the Worke," &c.   Johnson's reading, "*In Favour's* like," is commonly adopted; but I prefer Capell's.   See foot-note 34. — In the third line, the old text has "Most *bloodie, fierie.*"   The correction is Walker's.

P. 70. **No, it is Casca; one incorporate**
        To our attempt. — So Walker.   The old text has *Attempts.* The confusion of plurals and singulars is especially frequent in this play.

P. 70.   **Good Cinna, take this paper,**
        And look you lay it in the prætor's chair,
        Where Brutus may best find it. — The original has "may *but* find it."   The correction was proposed by Professor Craik.

ACT II., SCENE I.

P. 74. **Is not to-morrow, boy, the Ides of March?** — The original reads "the *first* of March."   This evidently cannot be right, though it may be what the Poet wrote: for in Plutarch, *Life of Brutus*, North's translation, he read as follows: "Cassius asked him if he were determined to be in the Senate-house the *first* day of the month of March, because he heard say that Cæsar's friends should move the Council that day, that Cæsar should be called king by the Senate."   Nevertheless the whole ordering of dates in the play is clearly against the old reading; so that Theobald's correction must be accepted.

P. 75. My ancestor did from the streets of Rome

The Tarquin drive, &c. — So Dyce. The original has " my *Ancestors*." See page 53, note 39.

P. 75. Speak, strike, redress! — Am I entreated, then,

To speak and strike? — So Pope. The old text lacks *then*, which is needful to the metre, and helpful to the sense.

P. 76. Sir, March is wasted fourteen days. — So Theobald. The original has " *fifteene* dayes," which cannot be right, as the Ides fell on the fifteenth of March, and this is the day before the Ides.

P. 76. The genius and the mortal instruments
    Are then in Council; and the state of man,

Like to a little kingdom, &c. — So the second folio. The original has " the state of *a* man." Both sense and metre are evidently against this reading ; and Walker points out many like instances of *a* interpolated. — I am all but certain that we ought to read *conflict* instead of *council*. See foot-note 16.

P. 77. For if thou pass, thy native semblance on,

Not Erebus itself were dim enough, &c. — The original reads " For if thou *path*," &c. This has been defended by some, and several instances cited of the verb to *path;* but those instances are quite beside the mark, as they do not use the word in any such sense as would justify its retention here. Coleridge proposed *put*, Walker strongly approves it, and Dyce adopts it. This is certainly strong authority, still I cannot reconcile myself to such a use of *put*. Surely a man cannot be rightly said to *put on* his *native* looks ; though he may well be said to *put* them *off*, or to *keep* them on. On the other hand, to *pass* may very well mean to *walk abroad*, or to *pass the streets*, which is the sense wanted here. Of course, with this reading, " thy native semblance on " is the ablative absolute ; " thy native semblance *being* on."

P. 79. No, not an oath : if not the face of men,

The sufferance of our souls, the time's abuse, &c. — There has been much stumbling at the word *face* here ; I hardly know why,

Warburton reads *fate;* Mason proposed *faith*, Malone *faiths*, which latter seems much the best of the three, as it would mean the *plighted faith* of the conspirators.   See foot-note 24.

P. 82.   **This shall mark**
      Our purpose necessary, and not envious. — So Collier's second folio. The original has *make* instead of *mark*. The former can only be explained " make our purpose *seem* necessary," — a sense which the word will hardly bear, but which the context plainly requires.

P. 83.   **Yet I do fear him;**
      For, in th' ingrafted love he bears to Cæsar. — So Pope. The original lacks *do*.

P. 85. **He loves me well, and I have given him reason.** — So Walker. The original has *Reasons* instead of *reason*. See foot-note 48.

P. 87.   **And, upon my knees,**
      I charge you, by my once commended beauty, &c. — So Pope and Hanmer ; Walker, also, says, " I think, *charge.*" The original has " I *charm* you."

ACT II., SCENE II.

P. 91.   **The things that threaten me**
      Ne'er look but on my back; when they shall see
      The face of Cæsar, they are vanishéd. — The original has *threaten'd* instead of *threaten*, which seems fairly required by the con- text.   Walker's correction.

P. 91. **Fierce fiery warriors fought upon the clouds,**
      In ranks and squadrons and right form of war,
      Which drizzled blood upon the Capitol;
      The noise of battle hurtled in the air;
      Horses did neigh, and dying men did groan; &c. — In the first of these lines, the original has " *fight* upon the clouds," and, in the last, " Horses *do* neigh," — errors which the context readily corrects.

P. 93. We are two lions litter'd in one day, &c. — The original reads " We *heare* two lions." Theobald changed *heare* to *were;* but *are* is evidently the right word ; and so Capell.

P. 94. She dreamt to-night she saw my statua,

    Which, like a fountain, &c. — The original has *statue.* It appears that the word, though spelt *statue,* was sometimes used as a trisyllable, *statuë.* But it is certain that the Latin form *statua* was often used till long after Shakespeare's time. See foot-note 6.

P. 94. And these doth she apply for warnings and porténts

    Of evils imminent; &c. — So Hanmer. The original has " *And* evils" ; doubtless an accidental repetition of *And* from the line above.

ACT II., SCENE IV.

P. 99. *Enter* ARTEMIDORUS. — The original has " *Enter the Sooth-sayer.*" Rowe substitutes *Artemidorus,* and the change is thus justified by Tyrwhitt : "The introduction of the Soothsayer here is unnecessary, and, I think, improper. All that he is made to say should be given to Artemidorus ; who is seen and accosted by Portia on his passage from his first stand to one more convenient."

P. 100. None that I know will be, much that I fear may chance. — Dyce suspects, as he well may, that the words *may chance* are " an interpolation." Certainly both sense and metre would be better without them. Pope omits them.

ACT III., SCENE I.

P. 102.   **If this be known,**

  Cassius or Cæsar never shall turn back,

    For I will slay myself. — White and Professor Craik substitute *on* for *or;* very injudiciously, I think. The change was proposed by Malone, with the remark that "the next line strongly supports this conjecture" ; whereupon Ritson comments as follows : "He must mean, it is presumed, in the Irish way ; as a mere English reader would conclude that the next line totally destroys it. Cassius says, if the plot be discovered, at all events either he or Cæsar shall never return alive; for, if the latter cannot be killed, he is determined to slay himself. The sense is as plain, as the alternative is just and necessary, or the proposed reading ignorant and absurd."

P. 102. **Popilius Lena speaks not of our purpose.** — The original has *purposes*. But Cassius has just said, "I fear our *purpose* is discoveréd." Corrected by Theobald.

P. 103. *Casca*. **Are we all ready?** — So Collier's second folio. The original makes this question the beginning of Cæsar's next speech. Ritson thought it should be given to one of the conspirators; and Cinna has just said, "Casca, you are *the first* that rears your hand."

P. 104. **And turn pre-ordinance and first decree**
        Into the play of children. — The original has *lane* instead of *play;* a very palpable blunder. The correction is Mason's. Johnson proposed *law*, and several have adopted that reading. But what is "the *law* of children"? To be sure, *lane*, in manuscript, looks more like *law* than like *play;* but I do not see that this amounts to much.

P. 104. *Met.* **Cæsar, thou dost me wrong.**
        Cæs. **Cæsar did never wrong but with just cause,**
        Nor without cause will he be satisfied. — I here restore a genuine piece of the Poet's text as preserved and authenticated to us by Ben Jonson. Instead of the three lines here quoted, the folio has only a line and a half, thus: "Know, Cæsar doth not wrong, nor without cause will he be satisfied." Jonson, in his *Discoveries*, speaking of Shakespeare, has the following: "Many times he fell into those things could not escape laughter: as when he said in the person of Cæsar, one speaking to him, 'Cæsar, thou dost me wrong,' he replied, 'Cæsar did never wrong but with just cause,' and such like; which were ridiculous." Jonson's personal and professional relations with Shakespeare gave him every possible opportunity of knowing that whereof he speaks. But, as compared with his great friend, he was something of a purist in language; and his censure in this case has long seemed to me rather captious. At all events Shakespeare repeatedly

uses *wrong,* both noun and verb, in the sense of to *hurt,* to *offend,* to *cause pain.* See foot-note 10. He seems to have been acquainted with the etymological relationship of *wrong, wring,* and *wrest.* In the text, Metellus uses *wrong* in the ordinary sense ; Cæsar, in the sense of to *hurt,* to *wring,* or to *punish.* Besides, the passage, as it stands in the folio, carries in its face evident marks of mutilation : the words, "Cæsar doth not wrong," &c., come in abruptly, and without any proper occasion : hence Gifford justly supposed the Poet to have written as in the text. As given in the folio, the word *satisfied* also seems quite out of place ; at least Cæsar has no apparent reason for using it. But, in the passage as censured by Jonson, that word comes in naturally, and in perfect dialogical order ; the meaning being, "Cæsar did never *punish* without just cause, nor without cause will he be satisfied *in the matter of punishment,* or *so as to revoke the sentence.*" How, then, came the passage to be as the folio gives it ? This question of course cannot be definitively answered. As Jonson had some hand in getting up the folio, it is nowise unlikely that he may have made the alteration ; though it would seem as if he might have seen that the change just spoilt the Poet's dramatic logic. Or it may well be that the Editors, not understanding the two senses of *wrong,* struck out the words *but with just cause,* and then altered the language at other points in order to salve the metre. Either of these is, I think, much more probable than that Shakespeare himself made the change in order to "escape laughter." At all events, Jonson is better authority as to how Shakespeare wrote the passage, than the folio is, that Shakespeare himself made the change. — Such being the case, I can offer no apology for the reading given in the text. I have already cited Gifford's opinion in the matter. Halliwell has in substance expressed a like judgment. And Dr. Ingleby avows it as his conviction, that the line which Jonson and his fellow-censors "laughed at was and is unimpeachable good sense, and that it is the editor's duty to use Jonson's censure for the purpose of correcting the folio reading."

P. 108. *Casca.* **Why, he that cuts off twenty years of life Cuts off so many years of fearing death.** — Some modern editors transfer this speech to Cassius ; but why? Surely it is more characteristic of Casca than of Cassius. And I am the more unwilling to take it from Casca, as it is the last he utters.

P. 108.   **How many ages hence**
            Shall this our lofty scene be acted o'er
    In States unborn and accents yet unknown!—The orig-
inal has *over* instead of *o'er*, and *State* instead of *States*. Walker says,
"The flow requires *o'er*. *Over* for *o'er* is a frequent error of the folio."
The other correction was made in the second folio.

P. 108. **That now on Pompey's basis lies along.**—So the second folio. The first has *lye* instead of *lies*.

P. 111. **To you our swords have leaden points, Mark Antony:**
         Our arms in strength of amity, and our hearts
    Of brothers' temper, do receive you in, &c.—The orig-
inal reads, "Our armes in strength of *malice*";* from which no con-
gruent sense can possibly be gathered. Many other changes have
been made or proposed, the best of which hitherto given is, I think,
Capell's,—"our swords have leaden points, Our arms *no* strength of
malice;" &c. But the logic and rhythm of the passage seem to require that the words "Our arms," &c., should be construed with what
follows, not with what precedes; for which cause I have never been
fully satisfied with Capell's reading. The reading in the text is Singer's. Collier has lately proposed "strength of *manhood*"; which seems
to me exceedingly apt and happy; but *amity*, if not better in itself,
involves less of literal change, and has more support from other passages of Shakespeare. So in *Antony and Cleopatra*, ii. 6: "That
which is the *strength of their amity* shall prove the immediate author
of their variance."

P. 112.   **And here thy hunters stand,**
    Sign'd in thy spoil, and crimson'd in thy death.—So
Pope, Theobald, and Collier's second folio. Instead of *death*, the original has *Lethee*, which is commonly printed *lethe*. Capell says that
lethe here is "a term used by hunters, to signify the blood shed by a
deer at its fall, with which it is still a custom to mark those who come
in at the death."

P. 114. **And that we are contented Cæsar shall**
    Have all due rites and lawful ceremonies.—So Pope,
Walker, and Collier's second folio. The original has *true* instead of *due*.

P. 115. **Woe to the hands that shed this costly blood!** — The original has *hand* instead of *hands*. But Antony says to the stabbers a little before, "whilst your purpled *hands* do reek," &c.

P. 115. **A curse shall light upon the limbs of men.** — It is quite amazing how much has been done, to help this innocent passage: as changes made and proposed, in order to get rid of *limbs*, we have *kind*, *line*, *loins*, *lives*, *times*, *tombs*, *sons*, and *minds*. If any change be necessary, I should say *souls*, which, beginning with the long *s*, might easily be misprinted *limbs*. But what need of change? See footnote 40.

P. 116. **Passion, I see, is catching; for mine eyes,**
    Seeing those beads of sorrow stand in thine,
    Begin to water. — The original has *from* instead of *for*, and *Began* instead of *Begin*; — palpable errors, both.

ACT III., SCENE II.

P. 119.   **Cæsar's better parts**
    Shall now be crown'd in Brutus. — So Pope. The original lacks *now*.

P. 119. **Do grace to Cæsar's corpse, and grace his speech,**
    Tending to Cæsar's glory. — The original has "Cæsar's *Glories*." Corrected by Walker. Brutus has just said "his *glory* not extenuated."

P. 122. **If thou consider rightly of the matter,**
    Cæsar has had great wrong.
       3 Cit.   **Has he not, masters?** — The original lacks *not*. Inserted by Professor Craik. Walker says, "Perhaps we should read 'Has he, *my* masters?'"

P. 126. **For I have neither wit, nor words, nor worth, &c.** — So the second folio. The first has *writ* instead of *wit*.

P. 129. **I heard 'em say, Brutus and Cassius**
    Are rid like madmen through the gates of Rome. — The original reads "I heard *him* say."

ACT III., SCENE III.

P. 129. **I dreamt to-night that I did feast with Cæsar,**
       And things unlucky charge my fantasy. — So Warburton.
The original has *unluckily* instead of *unlucky*. Walker says, "undoubt-
edly *unlucky*." See foot-note 1.

ACT IV., SCENE I.

P. 133. **A barren-spirited fellow; one who feeds**
       On objects, arts, and imitations,
       Which, out of use and staled, &c. — Theobald and, after
him, Dyce read " *abject orts* and imitations." This is, to me, little less
than shocking. It is true, Shakespeare uses both *abject* and *orts ;* and
I presume we all know the meaning of both those words : but is it
credible that he could have been guilty of such a combination as
abject orts ? Besides, does not the word *imitations* show that he had
in mind *works of art ?* And why may not *objects* stand for any common objects of interest or curiosity? The Clarendon edition prints
" *abjects, orts* and imitations"; which is certainly no improvement on
Theobald's reading. As to the objections urged against the old reading, I can but say they are to me only not quite so absurd as the
changes they are made to cover. See foot-note 7.

P. 134. **Therefore let our alliance be combined,**
       Our best friends made, our means stretch'd out. — So the
first folio, with the exception of the word *out*. The second folio makes
a full line, such as it is, thus : " Our best friends made, *and* our *best*
means stretch'd *out*." Neither reading is satisfactory, and modern
editors are, I believe, about equally divided between the two.

ACT IV., SCENE II.

P. 135.   **Your master, Pindarus,**
       In his own charge, or by ill officers, &c. — So Hanmer and
Warburton. The old text has *change* instead of *charge*. The latter
word, it seems to me, does not give the right sense ; and we have
many instances of *change* and *charge* misprinted for each other.

P. 136. **Lucius, do you the like ; and let no man**
    Come to our tent till we have done our conference. —
    Lucilius and Titinius, guard the door. — Here, in the orig-
inal, the names Lucius and Lucilius got shuffled each into the other's
place ; and then, to cure the metrical defect in the third line, that line
was made to begin with *Let.* Modern editors generally have rectified
the metre of the first line by striking out *you,* — " Lucilius, do the
like," &c. But this leaves things quite wrong in regard to the persons ; for Lucilius is an officer of rank ; yet he is thus put to doing
the work of what we call an orderly, while Lucius, the orderly, or
errand-boy, is set in the officer's place. We are indebted to Professor
Craik for rectifying this piece of disorder. — In the third line, the
original reads " guard *our* door." Probably an accidental repetition
of *our* from the line above. Corrected by Rowe.

ACT IV., SCENE III.

P. 137. **Whereas my letters, praying on his side**
    Because I knew the man, were slighted off. — Instead
of *Whereas,* the original has *Wherein,* which cannot easily be made to
yield a fitting sense.

P. 137. **And let me tell you, Cassius, you yourself**
    Are much condemn'd to have an itching palm. — So
Capell. The original is without *And* at the beginning of the speech.
Other editors have supplied *Yet.* Some such insertion is fairly required
for the prosody.

P. 138. **I had rather be a dog, and bay the Moon,**
    Than such a Roman.
      Cass.   **Brutus, bay not me, &c.** — Instead
of the second *bay,* the original reads *baite,* which has the same meaning indeed ; but probably, as Dyce says, " the author intended Cassius
to echo the word used by Brutus." The correction is Theobald's.

P. 138.   **I am a soldier, ay,**
    Older in practice, abler than yourself, &c. — So Steevens.
The original reads " I am a Souldier, *I,*" &c. The affirmative particle

ay is there very often printed *I;* and such I think is the case here; for the repetition of the pronoun *I* seems awkward and unnatural.

P. 140.   **For mine own part,**
I shall be glad to learn of abler men. — So Collier's second folio. The original has " of *Noble* men." As Cassius has in fact used the word *abler*, there can, I think, be little scruple about the correction.

P. 142. **A flatterer's would not, though they did appear**
           As huge as high Olympus. — So Collier's second folio. The original has " though they *do* appear."

P. 143.   **Yes, Cassius; and henceforth,**
When you are over-earnest with your Brutus, &c. — The original reads " and *from* henceforth." Here *from* is palpably redundant both in metre and in sense. Shakespeare probably wrote *from hence*, and then corrected the latter word into *henceforth;* and both got printed together. Capell omits *from*.

P. 148. **Come on refresh'd, new-aided, and encouraged.** — So Dyce and Singer. The original has *new added* instead of *new-aided*. Collier's second folio has " new-*hearted*."

P. 149. **Lucius, my gown! — Farewell now, good Messala:—**
           Good night, Titinius: &c. — The original is without *now*. Some such insertion is required for the metre. Hanmer printed " *Now*, farewell," and Walker says, " Perhaps *fare you well*."

P. 150. **Varro and Claudius!** — Here, and again afterwards, in the text, as also in the stage-directions, the original has *Varrus* and *Claudio*. There is, I believe, no doubt that the right names are *Claudius* and *Varro*. As before noted, *Flavius* and *Octavius* are repeatedly misprinted *Flavio* and *Octavio*.

ACT V., SCENE I.

P. 156. **Whilst damnèd Casca, like a cur, behind**
           Struck Cæsar on the neck. O flatterers! — The original has " O *you* Flatterers." Reasons of prosody caused *you* to be struck out long ago; but some recent editors restore it.

P. 158. Be thou my witness that against my will,
   As Pompey was, I am compell'd to set
   Upon one battle all our liberties. — The original inverts the
order of *I am*. But "be witness that *am I* compell'd" is not an English construction. Corrected by Walker.

P. 158. Coming from Sardis, on our foremost ensign
   Two mighty eagles fell; &c. — Instead of *foremost*, the original has *former*, which is said to have been sometimes used in the
sense of *foremost*. But the passage cited as proving such a usage
seems to me irrelevant. The correction is Rowe's.

ACT V., SCENE III.

P. 167. Thou last of all the Romans, fare thee well! — Instead
of *Thou*, the original has *The*. The old abbreviations of *the* and
thou were often confounded. Corrected by Rowe.

P. 167. Come, therefore, and to Thassos send his body:
   His funerals shall not be in our camp,
   Lest it discomfort us. — The original has *Thassus* for *Thassos*. Corrected by Theobald. Properly it should be *Thasos ;* but
North's Plutarch has it *Thassos.* — Some have changed *funerals* to
funeral ; also, in the next scene but one, *hilts* to *hilt*. But *funerals*
and *hilts* are old forms of the singular in those words. See page 164,
note 6.

ACT V., SCENE IV.

P. 168. I'll tell the news. Here comes the general. — The
original reads " Ile tell *thee* newes." Pope's correction.

ACT V., SCENE V.

P. 172. I shall have glory by this losing day,
   More than Octavius and Mark Antony
   By their vile conquest shall attain unto. — The original
reads " By *this* vile conquest." Walker proposes *their*, and adds,
" The repetition seems awkward and un-Shakespearian."

Theme — Rise & fall of the conspiracy.
Subject — Friends & enemies of Caesar.
Purpose — To glorify Caesar.
Dramatic time 3 years